Towards the Restoration of Nigeria
Discussions and Analysis of Major Issues

Hadiza Wada, DBA

This work is dedicated to the memory of the listed individuals who enriched our intellectual discourse with sincere and genuine concern.

Dr. Bala Muhammed
Dr. Ibrahim Tahir
Dr. Yusuf Bala Usman

Copyright © 2010
Hadiza Wada

All rights reserved. No part of this publication may be reproduced in any form or by an electronic or mechanical means, including information storage and retrieval system, without prior written permission from the publisher.

ISBN 978-0-9846036-0-2

Cover Design by:

Author

Published by "The Optimist Voice" an online weekly magazine URL: www.theoptimistvoice.com

TABLE OF CONTENT

Chapters:

Preface: *(Foreword)*..vi

Introduction..ix

1. Africa: Did You Hear The Call?

    A Glimpse at African Present Image........................1

    The Importance of Image Demystifying....................6

2. Nigerian Economic Challenges 33

    (a) Defining the Most Urgent Socio-Economic

    Problems...33

    (b) Breathing Life into the Economy: Lessons

    from Japan and China......................................51

    (c) Industrial Challenges....................................57

3. Nigerian Electrical Challenges and

    Solutions.. 68

4. Nigeria's Forgotten Heroes: Lessons Lost?.................82

    (a) Sa'adu Zungur... 82

    (c) Murtala Muhammad 86

5. Nigerian Political Challenges..................................... 102

    (a) The Rotational Presidency Quagmire 102

    (b) Nigeria at a Crossroad 112

    (c) Other Issues of Neglect...................................116

    (d) Defining the Root Issue of Budget

    Implementation 120

6. Nigerian Security Challenges.....................................128

    (a) Reversing Decades of Deterioration 128

   (b) Addressing Police Inefficiency.................................133
   (c) Niger Delta Issue: Not that Enigmatic 139
7. Recognizing Leadership Potential................................ 156
8. Nigerian Educational Challenges................................. 163
   African Educational Challenges........................... 163
   Country Specific Solutions 173
9. Revisiting the Status of Women.................................. 183
10. Strategies for Revamping African Economies..................194

Preface

At no time in history has it become so extremely important to awaken a nation from its slumber, so it may realize and live up to its full potential. The work of building a nation falls on the shoulders of its people primarily. Any other person that does not fall within that category can only assist. It is a duty and a responsibility regardless of the excuses that so many of us tender to ourselves and others to justify why, even after given a direct chance to make a contribution, a great number of the people continue to fail the nation.

This writer has come to a realization that if she does not make a direct contribution towards the solution, she cannot convince herself that she is not part of the problem. We are all mortal, and have a limitation to the length of time we have to make our contribution towards making our nation and our people, including our family and progeny live a deserving life. How else can we justify our life, education and resources made available to us through the bounties of our Lord?

When you get to a point where you feel ready to push ahead with such a task, you begin to tread the paths of those who have also made such efforts in the past. You feel that the effort is indeed achievable. Their spirits become alive, as you readily sense their eagerness, albeit limitations at their various times to get as much opportunities as you have. It is in that light that this writer dedicates her work to just some of those who stood out in that regard. They were enlightened people who sincerely wanted to share that light with their brethren, so they can together mould the nation's destiny to achieve a brighter future.

In the intellectual arena, Dr. Bala Muhammed was a beacon to whom people generally refer to as ahead of his time. I do not completely agree. He was on time. Nigeria should have developed way past where it is today, had people like him been taken seriously. The right information and education would have made the mob that put out that light early to the detriment of everyone, realize that he was working towards enlightening the young generation and the policy makers to work for the betterment of the country. Ignorance and hopelessness, the motivator of such a mob, is still one of the major impediments to development in the country today.

Dr. Yusuf Bala Usman and Dr. Ibrahim Tahir trod similar paths intellectually touching the lives of each student they taught, but their torches were shining for much longer. Their students are now professionals and policy makers in various sections of the country including abroad, making various contributions even if incrementally. But as with everyone else they were effectively limited by the same set of problems that plagued the nation. These are some of the problems we will try to present in this book. They have made their full contributions within the limits of their profession. These intellectuals' contributions coming to us through scholarly works all fall within the change through persuasion or "talking" arena, and that is the limitation. People have to rise up to the occasion and start "doing" for themselves. Generally, maintaining a good intention is good, discussing and agreeing to its merit better, but the best of all is acting upon such righteous deeds that are needed for the good of all.

Then there were also, in the political arena, trail blazers living and dead. This book hopefully brings to life their passion and message for the nation. They lived and some even gave the ultimate sacrifice to the nation, their lives. Some lived for their ideals, never wavering or getting distracted, as is so common today, by abandoning what is right for the accumulation of wealth. It is the writers hope that she captures their message and spirit in this book also, so as to awaken the nation to such laudable ideals for which they lived and died. To them we dedicate a chapter titled Nigerian Forgotten Heroes: Lessons Lost? We believe their ideas should not die with them. No nation progresses without taking and incorporating lessons that worked for it in the past.

What then are some of the reasons why Nigeria's progress helps not just the nation but the wider society? There are many such reasons. The sheer population of this pivotal nation of Africa makes it more expedient to set it on the right course. A nudge to put Nigeria on a path to success may benefit the whole continent, giving that it is one of the three most relevant in international politics, the other two continental colleagues being South Africa and Egypt. A growing power for Nigeria means a greater voice for African affairs.

What this writer noted, when it comes to Nigeria and its persistent problems, is that not much attention has been given the importance of deep analysis and documentation of national issues for a greater proportion of the Nigerian public to educate themselves about what is important. And any nation that wants to develop has to have an active and participant citizenry. To achieve that, people have to be constantly informed about all important issues. Issues can neither be brushed under the carpet, nor important matters be made secret. While the government owes the public information about all its activities which should be in the national interest, and how it is spending the nation's resources, the people also have equal responsibility to make efforts in staying informed about all important matters that affect their lives, that of their children, family, and the nation in general. So follow the issues keenly and carefully. When they get derailed, call to order. If you do not have the influence for enforcement, persuade someone who has, to do it for the good of all.

More important is the ability to sincerely distinguish and fully recognize areas where the government will not suffice, then coming together with ideas where the citizens themselves can take it up and make it work. Such areas include education. Presently politicians use the issue in point scoring, without seriously acknowledging that quality education needs the assistance of everyone including parents, elders, interest groups, non-governmental organizations, endowments, foundations and other avenues to effectively work.

Finally, all institutions responsible for keeping people informed and educated enough to make the critical decision possible and in a timely fashion have to be used. These include the nation's schools, mass media, journals, public libraries etc. Presently, the Nigerian press, though important to the nation's development and information dissemination, does a lot of harm in my personal opinion, especially in drumming divisive and counterproductive issues, while letting important issues pass unnoticed and un-discussed. We pray that this work also adds its voice to such need for positive enlightenment.

Hadiza Isa Wada, DBA
March 30, 2010

Introduction

My sincere goal for undertaking this project is to impart and cultivate a thorough understanding of issues for Nigerians in an effort to stimulate and motivate them towards becoming proactive citizens who will initiate genuine and important demands of their leaders based on prevailing facts and records. Development and prosperity, we believe, can only be accelerated when people stop reacting to what is thrown at them and begin a sincere study of what is required, tabling it before their governmental representatives and demanding that they be provided. As for the leadership, what is principally required of them is maintaining the moral bearing and the political courage to act right for the people they swore to work for. Justice and righteousness demand that leaders sincerely serve the electorate within their immediate jurisdiction. No one should tolerate "Uncle Toms" whose primary interest is to please those invisible foreign hands thousands of miles across the ocean who made their 'selection" possible, regardless of their incompetence. And who oppress their local population, pursuing other less important interests, neglecting issues of life and death that plague the electorate. The nation and its people in general is what needs to be saved and developed, regardless of whose bull is gored, or whose intrigues are exposed.

Such issues however as we have witnessed, is not in the political radar of the typical leaders or politicians, but the sensibilities of their individual, political, or party patrons and powerbrokers. So if they choose not to do the right thing in tackling what issues plague the nation, our prayer is that an informed citizenry will force them towards the right thing they want from them. And if they refuse to listen, find a way to get rid of them and replace them with the right people.

Finally, it could be the source of genuine debates which will unearth more issues, inspire more ideas and motivate people towards solving them. Likewise, it is intended to inspire debate and discussions among citizen from all walks of life. Such debates should not be limited to politicians and schools only as is commonly practiced. No group has a monopoly on ideas. So we intend and will work towards encouraging such debates and churning of ideas on important issues that plague the nation to extend to all people while riding in their cars, or herding and farming in the wild, and across the table in offices, businesses, markets stalls, restaurants and all walks of life.

But my deepest desire is to enlighten and motivate the population of Northern Nigeria who in my opinion are the most passive. They are becoming increasingly passive, probably owing to the present situation since the return of civilian administration in 1999. Since 1999, the population of Northern Nigeria have forcefully been denied their rights as a majority to shape decision making and the political future of the country, a right every majority group have enjoyed across the world.

This position was achieved through carefully worked out schemes, intrigues and especially, last minute changes in policy by a political party that has already captured more national attention than any other political party at that time. The result was an eight years stretch of an administration that has made issues such as the security of lives and property a non issue. And we know that without peace, not much can be accomplished in terms of prosperity.

And because there is some vested interest for long to bring about the same game plan for oppressing the majority and vilifying them, the party has used all means at its disposal to remain in power long enough to entrench and maintain that undemocratic and dictatorial tendency to oppress a majority and snatch by force its constitutional rights. Ironically this is being done in the name of democratic ideals, but actually what we have been witnessing is quite the opposite.

A lot of casualties have emerged from that exercise, beyond regional borders. The country as a whole now suffers many ailments as a result of such narrow-minded ideology. Party leaders including self serving northern elites continue to engage in a political gamble, battering their property, future and survival of the nation on a political table. As a result people have been loosing their lives in large numbers for a decade.

The majority, being a positive attribute in any democratic system, has suddenly become a curse for residents of Northern Nigerian today. They have been made victims largely with the assistance of Nigerian subjective Press and are gradually loosing grips on what is happening around them. The resulting effect has also forced the ship of state to steer off course. I may not have to convince any reader, aware of Nigerian situation today, that a dire need exists to set things right, in order to diffuse the tension, insecurity, political puzzle and mistrust that resulted from a decade of such misdirection.

Another very crucial attitude that needs to be reversed as soon as possible is the introduction into the psyche of the nation that political leadership and success can only be attained and maintained through cruel and tyrannical cultish practices. People who profess Islam and Christianity openly do not appear to believe inwardly that their God is able to assist them. They therefore buy into the belief that one has to lean towards the darker forces, to ensure his participation and maintenance of power.

Others with vested interest in spreading mischief have used that weakness in faith to their advantage. The result today is the insensitivity to loss of human lives in heinous manners and ways that we witness daily. The sacredness of human life is increasingly becoming irrelevant, a precedent that will not augur well for anyone consequently, including those who today are thinking they maintain the upper hand. History has taught us that, once you let the genie out of the bottle, or as they say when you light a fire and allow it to burn out of control in the same surrounding with you, your loved ones, and the so called "my people" (which in most cases is actually for political expediency), you may not possess the ultimate power to control who it affects, and who it will ultimately consume.

The irony is, more than eighty percent of Nigerians who profess following the two major religions practiced in the country know better, but that is no reason to abandon their chosen destructive path. While we clearly learn in unambiguous terms that Prophet Isa (Jesus) on him be peace, fought such evil and even casted such forces out of his followers. And also that the teacher for the Muslims, Prophet Muhammad in unambiguous terms warned his followers against the devil, his practices and his evils, people still somehow believe that it is their one and only means to success in politics and leadership seeking ambition. They therefore abandon their Mosques and Churches, to head to the shrines and cultic centers. With the result that ordinary Nigerians dread times of political activism around elections, for these are times that kidnapping, ritual killings and such practices become rampant.

Finally, we hope to also encourage many more people with adequate skills in researching, investigating and writing to begin to take serious the process of putting things in writing and emanating ideas on issues of importance. Oral tradition that we have inherited from our cultures may have influenced our over reliance on orally passing on information to the upcoming generation being born every single day. But with today's various complexities, including an ever plaguing subjective news coverage, issues may continue to be buried along with the genuine avenues of addressing them. Otherwise Nigeria is no different from any other nation, and therefore its problems should not be any more difficult to solve.

Recommending solutions is also our goal

Just as our weekly online magazine logo "we speak the truth and Provide solutions" another goal is providing solutions or ways to reach such solutions. The project we conceived a year ago, works along the same lines. We are dedicated to presenting serious articles that will set the agenda, as opposed to reacting to issues when they surface. This we did because we believe that Nigerian problems are not insurmountable.

Every nation has the ability to move forward as long as it is willing to find out its major challenges, publicize them, discuss them and finally set out with the dedication needed to finding lasting solutions. In general therefore this book becomes a must read for every dedicated Nigerian, politician, students across the nation and others who just want a good understanding of Nigerian issues today. It will also be useful to non Nigerians, and such groups will include, for example, diplomatic officials, students of African History, foreign relations agents, and scholars. It may also clarify for donors with genuine intentions in helping the country, find legitimate causes and decide where to direct their funds etc

Before we delve into this work, we would like to recognize some underlying causes responsible for some negative consequences we observe in Northern Nigeria. They are a people who understandably are making the most adjustment to a system of government (Western style democracy) that in contemporary terms have been developed in nations that have a wide cultural variance with its inhabitants values. As if that is not enough a challenge, these are the people whose opinions you hardly hear because they own just a unitary percentage of the nation's press (less than ten percent) while they are by far the majority in head count. They read less in terms of Western style press and print, and conduct a lesser percentage of serious researches about their daunting problems far less than any other group.

In the present Nigerian psyche, the nation, its leadership (politicians and otherwise) as well as the press, inhabitants of Northern Nigeria are stereotyped as "Muslim North." The second specialized categorization "Hausa Fulani," though glaringly inaccurate owing to the fact that there are many more ethnic groups and languages living in that general area, is another term of reference adopted. Whether viewing the area as one inhabited by a Muslim majority made others see it in ethnic terms as well (Hausa Fulani); or the reverse of that i.e. the majority of its inhabitants are Hausa Fulani made others see it in religious terms as well is something we could leave for others to fine tune with deeper research. For the information of our casual reader, the Hausa and Fulani are about ninety nine percent Muslims, the exception being very rare. They shared common history in the past and intermingled so much so that they have a common reference as a group today.

Having defined the typical Northern Nigerian in contextual terms, we will say this; without sincerely addressing the challenges of that majority, we can only go down a road towards perdition, similar to other nations we observe today from afar. Failure to come to terms with the challenges of the majority population has led to anarchy in many nations of the world.

The most urgent of the problems

One key area is the growing dissatisfaction of Nigerian youths, who continue to see no light at the end of the tunnel, in terms of where their future lies. While they command a great percentage of Nigerian population, people are too engrossed in their schemes to give them a thought and the required attention needed to address their ever rising problems. Their parents are increasingly moving towards self defeating goals, where the primary goal is not community based but personal aggrandizement and greed in piling ill gotten wealth. They spend a great number of years schooling, but since the educational system is also problem prone, they graduate without adequate education to make them productive members of the society. They end up becoming a burden to themselves, and the community at large.

The non involvement of youths in anything tangible translates into a great waste of talent and manpower, for the youth are the most energetic and daring; with abilities to inject energy into the industrial, agricultural, and all other facets of development in any country. Any nation that does not find a way to harness that energy will run at a great loss. Because Nigerian youths could not channel such energy and enthusiasm positively, they have become easy to incite to cause mayhem. The reality you may get from people who have studied human developmental stages is, that energy the youths have will have to be used up in one way or another. You have a choice as their leaders to draw up a plan to harness and direct that latent energy for developmental purposes, or else you leave them wandering without work and adequate guidance and they will use that energy destructively.

The generation above the youths i.e. their parent's generation, who would have been more involved in leadership and governance were not opportune to be genuine role models. Those in their mid forties to about sixty years of age, have not been given adequate chances to get involved with their contributions at the epic of power. Mostly the same people since independence have been recycled at federal level leadership positions such as Presidents, Ministers, heads of major governmental companies and parastatals. Nigeria being half a century old this year, means the people who have refused to give way, who may have been in their thirties and above at independence are now in their eighties and above, and still seeking to remain in power. Even governorship at state level has not return to people of mid age until recently. The result is what appears to keep dragging the nation into the same old age dogmas of ethnic differences, regional differences, political hooliganism and the rest which are age old political gimmicks.

Then comes one of the most serious threats to the present round of democratic government; i.e. the global propaganda aimed particularly at people of the Islamic faith. It provides the avenue for some misdirected appointed and elected leaders to justify some tyrannical and irresponsible agenda of ethnic cleansing. The Hausa speaking Muslim today is a target of constant campaign of killing and elimination. Today Nigerians of Islamic faith have seen massacres you may term living hell. For example there was the 2004 massacre, where Muslims at Yelwan-Shendam and several remote villages and towns of Plateau State, though not the first incident, were massacred in front of their families, while others within single families were separated forever. This has unfortunately become part of the history of the Nigerian nation. And since then several other incidents have occurred, some glaringly incited by the leadership of Plateau state. That was something you may have thought is impossible to find occurring in the twenty first century anywhere in the world.

The menace though fanned by local ethnic hatred, has some foreign support that encourages it unfortunately. Nigeria is now experimenting with U S style democratic system, and has therefore on many occasions taken cues and lessons from historical and contemporary U S issues and policies. The last decade when Nigeria began its democratic experimentation, coincides with the previous George Bush Jr., Republican Administration, which even internally in the United States soon became quite unpopular. Reasons for the administration's failures are as diverse as there are writers to etch their opinions in several New York Times best sellers. But one popular overriding criticism is aggression.

Some conspiracy theorists have opined that the Bush Jr. administration 2000-2008 in the United States tried to implement the Bush Sr. idea of a New World Order, which as it unfolds have revealed that the new targeted enemy worldwide is the Muslim, his faith and people. This issue appears to further complicate Nigeria's problem. After initial bursts of ethnic crisis the country witnessed from 1999 onwards, the year the country returned to democratic rule, the crisis soon turned into a religious one. The first of such crisis occurred in October 1999 at Shagamu, a suburban area of Lagos generally populated by Northern Hausa speaking merchants and their families for generations. That was essentially an ethnic crisis, where the majority Yoruba in the city rose against inhabitants of northern origin generally, and Hausa Muslims within its midst in particular. Such crisis gradually spread to other areas, but was generally confined to the first political term which ended in 2003. Thereafter the crisis turned religious and affected much more cities, particularly Kaduna and Jos, two Northern States with sizable Christian populations, and a long history of religious tolerance and coexistence. Today, after the return of democratic governments eleven years ago, there have been more incidents of religious crisis than at anytime in the nation's history.

There is a pointer to what seemed to have materialized within the administration of Olusegun Obasanjo that connects with the New World Order scheme. You might recall that as soon as Obasanjo's candidacy for PDP was announced, the retired army general referred to himself as a "born again Christian." While the nation was working towards returning to democratic dispensation after the sudden death of General Sani Abacha and the announcement of his successor General Abdulsalami Muhammad that he intends to stay in power briefly to within a year (12 months period) prepare the country for democratic elections, something happened. At a critical time during that preparation, invisible hands from without and visible ones from within seem to have forced on the nation the candidacy of the Retired General Olusegun Obasanjo.

Before then, the Retired General and soon to be its president has been confined to the walls of a prison cell along with his colleagues that include the late Tafidan Katsina Shehu Musa 'Yar Adua, a brother to the late Nigerian President Umar Musa 'Yar Adua. They were jailed in connection with what was announced as their involvement with a failed coup attempt against the administration of General Sani Abacha. At the time that people were contemplating Obasanjo Presidential candidacy, some see him as a moderate leader drawing from the nation's first experience with his leadership after the assassination of General Murtadha Muhammad.

But others correctly opined that the Retired General Obasanjo may not be that moderate, especially owing to the fact that the first round of leadership was circumstantial, filling a position left for him after the sudden death (assassination) of General Murtadha. And that he may prove otherwise due to his vengeful and unforgiving nature, where he never forgets to pay back those he believed have crossed his lines. To think he just came out of prison is a warning signal. His first experience as a leader, they say, is different from another round where from the beginning the nation is entrusting him with such authority through a democratic form of government soon after leaving prison. In Obasanjo, the foreign agenda appears to have found a willing ally.

Foreign Influence

Many books have been written within the past decade in an attempt to disclose to the world what may be happening to global policy of the world's most formidable power, the United States. Under the administration of George Bush Jr., a lot happened that set a different tone, when it comes to diplomatic connection between different nations of the world and the United States, and most telling is the administration's policy towards most Islamic nations, and even those that have Islamic majority. The result was bad and sometimes catastrophic for Nigerians. As most of the adult population especially the elite tow the line just as their leader, succumbing to many values at variance with local values without any debate or contemplation, some of the population with less to lose began to seek a different path. Either a result of, or influenced by, or else a separate offshoot to the continued internal moral decay and external pressure from propaganda, the nation began to see the emergence of Islamic youth groups with a completely separate and unique social and religious ideology on life. Such groups include the Boko Haram and Dar-ul-Islam. Probably desperate for a working philosophy on life, adherents to these new forming groups moved off the prevailing social order they abhor, coming up with their own alternatives.

Here we would like to clarify that though most people tend to think that the attack on the World Trade Center in the year 2001 was the reason for that campaign and media propaganda against Islamic countries, that was not the case. The sudden and abrupt end to the cold war, or rivalry between countries of the Western World and those of the East was the cause. Most scholars discuss the underlying reality that since the fall of the communist Eastern block of nations under the WARSAW security pact (with the Soviet Union as its leader), and the arguable triumph of the democratic nations of NATO under the leadership of the United States, the victor has desperately sought another adversary to target and chase in line with the old order of dividing the world into two camps. Islam became the chosen adversary unfortunately. Since the late eighties and the early nineties books were written about that idea notable among them is Professor Samuel Huntington's "The Clash of Civilizations." So the idea of a new world order of the early nineties, and that of "clash of civilizations" preceded the attack by years.

This is a revived tactic however, not an entirely new idea. Students of history will tell you that earlier campaigns and propaganda against followers of Islam just seem to fade in some eras and rise in others. Writing as far back as 1979, Madni Abbasi in his book titled "The Family of the Holy Prophet" has some interesting things to say about the situation of Islamic countries and the challenges they face. Thirty years ago, he accurately predicted the era we are living in at present.

In the preface to his book, Abbasi expounded on the problems describing how the older religious order of the people of the book has sought to malign the religion since its early days in an effort to (a) discredit it so people may not give attention to the message that has a potential of freeing them from feudalistic grip of fascist political leaders and feudal religious clergy, who assign to themselves positions of power, authority and worship, beyond those sanctioned by their books, and turning their followers into virtual worship of them, as the saints are appointed and prayed to even as we speak today. In Islam the individual is empowered and encouraged to pray directly to God one-on-one at any clean place he could find. There is no need to go through an intercessor, who may exert some overbearing burden on an individual.

The second reason (b) he tabled was the persistent struggle and grudge against Muslims for their inhabiting and control of Khyber and Jerusalem which people of earlier scriptures view as a reminder from the Sultan Salahuddin conquest of the area. Abbasi continues by saying "Ever since then, they have not missed any opportunity to harm the Muslims or ridicule them...they never tolerated any powerful Muslim state and tried their best to dismember it as in the case of Turkish Empire. They helped Pakistan's enemies to cut it into two, and are now intriguing to further weaken it...In Nigeria they tried their best to create the State of Biafra...They are after Iran in the guise of checking the proliferation of atomic bombs." It has been thirty years since the publication of the book, but Abbasi is citing what up until today is an issue and a policy. He writes "they are trying their best not to allow any Muslim state to have even atomic reactors for generating power."

The global religious campaign and its effect on Nigerian Muslims

Before we delve into this topic, it is important to note that though many people think that as a Christian nation people in the United States may back religious extremists or zealots parading themselves as messiahs for political expediency in Nigeria, that is not so. That idea is not common place, or as they will call it in the United States, mainstream. A great majority of African Americans, for example, regardless of religious affiliation do not buy into the policy of the previous U S Administration that appear, regardless of countless interjections denying the idea, to target the Muslim as the enemy through military and media campaign. The very liberties and rights they fought hard and gained, with their sweat and blood were the same ones being compromised by the anti-Islamic rhetoric. Further, they know how it feels to target any group or individual for subjective, discriminatory, and inhumane reasons, and have kept their distance. A significant number of U S Catholics also feel the same. They also are subjected to discrimination because they are usually immigrant American minorities of Spanish lineage, from neighboring South American countries.

The problem emanates from some pockets of Southern Caucasian Christian extremist groups in the U S who usually are not mainstream. One of such groups was described by Chris Hedges (2007) as Dominionists. While Mark Miller (2004) does not provide any particular name, both descriptions say the goal is to establish a Fascist Christian Theocracy based in the U S but with a global outlook. Miller believes the former Bush Administration is closely aligned with the movement, hence the wars we saw despite unsubstantiated reports of WMD in Iraq, the radicalization of U S legal system and both foreign and domestic policy reformation.

Hedge says "Dominionsim is a fascist movement in that it emphasizes magic, leadership worship, and a belief in a master race, the Christian fundamentalist." "Jews are seen as a fallen evil people who killed Prophets and chose the material world over fulfilling God's covenant. And with the second coming of Christ the Jews along with all Muslims would be destroyed by Jesus." This quote is a summarized description from the review article in *The Muslim Link,* which reviewed and commented on the book in its January 7, 2010 issue.

While those groups have been in existence for many years, they were never allowed to play major roles if any in the political arena. The writers including many others have pointed to the previous administration as the first to not only give such sentiments an ear, but have given it a role to play. That was how some of the groups found their way into Iraq, and appear to influence some of the war policy. Strong evidences and close examination show that the middle belt perpetrators of violence in Nigeria share the same doctrine, and probably practical connections with the group.

Among U.S. groups closely aligned with the Dominionists are the Southern Methodists and Southern Baptist Convention, groups with long connections with the Nigerian Biafran war since the 1960s. These Southern Christian groups in the United States were the strongest advocates of black race enslavement and fought vehemently against its abolition. They are the states that minorities find the most difficult to live in to date. They went to war (civil war) with the industrializing Union States of the North to oppose the North's stance against continuing slavery, and to this day some of them fly their civil war flag of rebellion (the confederate flag).

What is curiously funny though, is trying to figure out why any African group or leader should follow the lead of a group that despises them as a people because of their race. Those who establish and lead the theocratic movement do not like Semites (Jews and Arabs) neither do they like people of color; black, yellow, brown, red and in between. They glorify chiefly the white race and only work with people of color willing to allow themselves to be used by them.

 So my advice to Nigerian victims of such perpetrated violence is, they owe it to themselves, and their media owe them also, important information that may continue to shed light on their government's sentiments. Information is power, they say. While keeping themselves informed and on guard about like movements worldwide, they should keep to their righteous path, in faith and not give up hope. Tables do turn as we have witnessed time and time again in History, and a time will definitely come when everyone who has openly perpetrated unjust deeds will be judged even while living in this world.

This position of God working for the oppressed is supported by all scriptures from God. God is so just, and holds one accountable only to the degree of his exigencies, no more no less. That is why even among our Christian brothers and sisters living in developed countries, you hear often in discussions about man's injustice to man that "when you dish out bad actions to someone else, make sure you can absorb the same abuse should it return on you, because surely it will return unto you sooner or later.

Lack of Leadership

If there is something the world has lost enough of, it is leadership. It has been a worldwide phenomenon for more than a decade. From the most powerful nation the United States, to most of the weaker ones in Africa, Asia and Arab world and South America; most of those in leadership positions were so much engrossed in themselves and their questionable values to think about the people they swore to defend and work for. They either were a problem in themselves, or feel obligated to follow the whims of stronger nations regardless of its impact on their own populations.

The irony was that, most of those governments in the industrialized nations tried hard through their control of global media and wars to convince the world that they are struggling to bring in a just world based on moral and religious principles. But the question many philosophical arguments and writers point to is whose justice and whose moral values are the parameters for such mass campaigns and wars? While some writers and non profit organizations point to a world control agenda in disguise, others point to an extremist religious agenda.

Mark Miller (2004), and Chris Hedges (2007) as we pointed earlier shed light on the extremist doctrine arm of the Iraqi war. Mark Miller at the time of his writing was a Professor of Media Studies from New York University, while Hedges was Harvard Divinity School Graduate who abandoned his chance of being ordained as a priest for journalistic causes. After spending 15 years as a correspondent for New York Times, he chose to resign from the newspaper because of its pro Iraqi war stance. He has since been honored with a Pulitzer Prize for his works. These are some of the people convinced that Christian extremist agenda will not augur well for the nation United States, their allies, or other nations across the ocean.

In short therefore, the challenges for Nigeria, though daunting appears to be both internal and external. Some of the most important challenges which we set out to address touch on very important and at times explosive problems. They range from political experimentation coupled with economic and social corruption. Also addressed are embezzlement and misappropriation of funds and neglect of people's basic interests. Security and energy problems are also featured, so also the social order that is rapidly changing to a less desirable one.

Chapter One

Africa: Did You Hear the Call?

A Glimpse at African Present Image

It is befitting, for the subject matter of this book to begin with this article, written by the writer in July 2005 during a musical tribute to raise funds for African victims of drought and poverty. The concert involving various world musicians tagged "Live 8" was conducted in all G8 states and South Africa and carried live via satellite across the world.

The rally for a moral cause earlier this month by famous musicians – Live 8 – once again brought the much needed spotlight on the African continent, even if for just a day. A continent so neglected by the whole world, and when I say the world I mean everyone, including its own people. The point is, while not belittling the efforts of those who spent their precious time and resources to arrange and participate in live 8, in reality that was just one of the 365 days in every calendar year. Reality sets in for the remainder of the 364 days of the year, for every one of those miserable African children and adults you saw that day.

Every continent on our planet, seven of them, each with its own personality lying across the beautiful blue planet called Earth today is the sibling of the rest of the continents. They all came into existence when the ocean waters receded to reveal land. Each of the continents nurses the children of one mother earth. But how do the other continents today view their sister continent Africa? If the answer is revealed by such worldly events, like live 8 then we all know the general picture. Whenever the spotlight shines on fundraising events for Africa, the pictures that stare us in the face are diseased, hungry and desolate people. Their glassy watery eyes speak to you, yet gazing past you in shear hopelessness. Their dry, frail, and fleshless skins were clinging to their bones as if in fear of undeserved and untimely demise - begging and pleading at your spirit for mercy - without the need for them to even open their mouths.

Is that the African fate? Was it born among its sibling continents, like the "Black" sheep of the family to just lie desolate, wasted and occupied by equally desolate and wasted people? Or should we believe that some kids of the same mother should be fed less, cared for less or even be allowed to be abused and neglected? Is every member of the family equally responsible for the care of every other member, or should we really hold the child itself responsible for its own fate? These are seemingly simple, yet complex questions that need to be addressed comprehensively, if we are interested in finding ways that will help the child become self-sufficient, able to grow and support itself.

To share with you my own view of the African continent is to share an experience that was so touching. My first air flight into the African continent after spending some time in the United States as a graduate student was an unforgettable experience that continues to repeat itself whenever I travel to the continent. My first experience brought tears to my eyes. And to this day with repeated travel mere memories bring back those same tears.

When the plane takes off from the United States as always, all the open fields one views from the sky whether cultivated or not, look luscious and green, full of life, spirit and beauty. Its greenery and serpentine rivers meandering through the pines, oaks, shrubs and brushes - gripping your staring eyes in an entertaining and inviting way. Even the mountains are either vegetated with dark green foliage seemingly singing in delight, and like every other living thing ever calling up to the Gracious Lord above with the hope of being fed with rain and abundant sunshine. Other mountains yet stand firm and bold, like the spirited soldier at full attention, caped by snow, ice or pregnant clouds floating and gliding like cotton balls of sparkling white, brushing the mountain caps in soothing reassurances of continuous support for survival.

Then you move onto the blue ocean for hours to, on most occasions a stop over somewhere in Europe. International travel from the United States usually begins in the evening crossing the Atlantic at night and arriving early morning mostly before sunrise in Europe. If arriving a city before twilight, you are immediately greeted by sparkling lights like dazzling diamonds in endless rows of different hues and patterns, a master jeweler's artistic and priceless work. The residents of the city sleep undisturbed by the noise, heat or cold weather outside. Uninterrupted electricity makes it possible to adjust the temperature of their homes to their comfort, while treated windows keep out all noises including that of the landing plane. If arriving by sunrise in the early morning hours, you are immediately welcomed by the gentle sway of the bright green grass as the breeze moves caressing its back in a reassuring wake up call. Sometimes fields of grain ready for harvest lay near the airport as if to reassure landing visitors of the abundance of food. Few minutes later you are landing on the tarmac and after a leg stretch hoisted back into the belly of another plane for a much shorter flight to Africa. That is the dreading part.

The short ride across the tip of the European land mass is usually for minutes then you cross the Mediterranean Sea. The agony comes when you begin to view the land of Africa. Like the "black" sheep of the family, it usually starts with a view of dark and dry smoldering mountains crouching bare under intense heat which makes you begin to wonder how those mountains have patiently stood there for years with their bare backs under direct hundred degree Fahrenheit temperature almost all year long without crying out in pain. In fact they are some of the most patient mountains, for they do not have a history of pouring out their hot melting guts in pain and rage.

African mountains are so jagged, rough and razor-back looking, probably from years of intense desert heat and chemical erosion. There appears no life around them, fauna or flora. So quiet, except may be for the roaring engine of the plane. Just like those faces from live-8, the mountains cry out to you without shedding their tears. They could not squeeze any even if they try. So in answer to their pain, I suddenly felt a burst of tears run down my cheeks. I wanted to pull the plane window shutters down, but just like the emotional yet curious child would, I could not gather the momentum for it. I had to share this painful moment with the voiceless mountains that are patiently standing tall, in intense pain and anguish.

Soon you move onto the sandy dunes of the Sahara. You immediately get some temporary relief looking at the sand. At least they seem to have some life I thought, compared to the Mediterranean mountain ranges. This is because, just like the sea, they are wavy. That tells you they do have some motion, changing their landscape with the blowing wind from time to time. But do they have life, I wonder. After all, the scientists say that movement alone though an important attribute of life, does not by itself prove life. As far as your eyes could see, thousands of feet above land, there is no vegetation to look up the heaven and make the plea for rain. There are no rivers or any sign of water. Not even the building clusters that you see once every few miles on other continents. No roads either, that would suggest the possibility of people going back and forth somewhere on the ground.

The picture is not much different across the Sahel, Sudan and Guinea Savanna region of Africa. Just minutes before the Nigerian border you begin to see negligble movement and some evidence of life but not much. As you land in Northern Nigeria, in the Guinea Savanna region, less than an hour flight to the shrinking rain forest by the southern Atlantic coast, all you see from far up above, is some dotted green specks. The rain forest of Africa is just a small percentage of the total land mass. As you land in the Savanna region, the trees are so far apart they look like the knotted hair of an African child (uncared for) suffering from ringworm, who has had his head shaven not long ago and ended up taking a swim in a stagnant pit of water. Or else the head of the vulture, if there is much hair up there.

All along I was asking myself, what is wrong with this picture. What is wrong with the continent of Africa? Is the African physical land mass responsible for its condition or the inhabitants on its back? Who should begin to make an all year round effort to put a mother continent, cradle of human civilization back on its feet once again? Should the African inhabitants alone be the ones burdened with the responsibility, or should they also rely on some of its most recent descendants in Diaspora? Should we also call on those that were once its children that ran off onto other continents, or should we absolve the lost child of any responsibility? When I say the lost children I mean the whole of human race that were, according to some controversial yet fully scientific study, genetically linked to the African mother?

What is hard to run away from is the reality that the human destiny is one. The earth is one, and all its continents are siblings. If as outsiders, we watch any human sibling treats its sister like this, we will jump to judgment quickly. Some, as we see in the contemporary world, may even jump and volunteer to adopt the neglected and abused child regardless of origin. Well Africa does struggle once in a while to speak out to the world, even if without a voice. But is anyone listening?

The Importance of Image Demystifying

Hadiza Wada, DBA …March 13, 2010

Introduction

Before we venture into the core issues we intend to raise and address, we start with this chapter titled "The Importance of Image Demystifying" because we believe it may set the right tone and attitude. We believe that a need exists to break the chains of mind control that has turned millions on the continent into people without self esteem, targeted based on race partially and also location (Africa). By self esteem we mean that their enthusiasm to help themselves has been castrated by a barrage of negativism which made them feel they cannot achieve no matter how hard they try. A result that has turned a whole continent into one that feels it could only survive either through others' sympathy in trade and commerce or else "aid." Many reasons account for this, but one of the most important weapons used to cause such apathy has to be targeted and shattered. And that is the mass campaign, explicit and tacit, conscious and subconscious, that creates negative images of a people, thereby effectively arresting their developmental potentials.

The most potent threat to contemporary status quo today is image reversal. We may not be the only group of people affected by image destruction, but we surely are the worst affected globally. The world has allowed itself to get caught up in a series of habitual ways of doing things politically, economically, socially and most importantly today, religiously. Cabals of a few worldly figures have found it expedient to promote certain values in these spheres to uphold the status quo, where about 5% of the world population control and manipulate more than ninety percent of world riches, throwing an increasingly bigger proportion of world population into financial difficulties, and more than fifty percent of them in poverty. One of the weapons, and as we say the most portent of them is the creation and sustaining of an image that serves their purpose.

You may think it is an exaggeration to assume today that half the world population of about seven thousand million (6,811,800,000 as of March 31, 2010) is estimated to be living in poverty, but that is true. These statistics are retrievable from various reliable sources, but you have to look for it, because no one will volunteer to tell you. To publicize it, is to go against the interests of those self-selected few, drawing the attention of the world to the real problems, thereby shining the spotlight on people responsible for them. Just a few months ago one of U S best selling authors, an economist (Perkins, 2009), described these statistical realities about the United States of America in his book "Hoodwinked" released in November 2009. He writes *"Do we want to raise our children on a planet where less than 5% of the population consumes more than 25% of the resources, less than 10% of that 5% control the assets, and roughly half of the world live in poverty?"*

The Role of Image

In our present times, image, whether rooted in reality or illusion is everything. It is all a question of perception. By this we mean how a vast majority of the world population view someone, something, a group, a nation or an idea. What kind of emotion gets aroused when the group, person, or nation is mentioned? Do you get a good positive feeling with the utterance of that name? Or is it your defenses and protective mechanism that immediately comes to the foreground. Do you feel motivated to learn what is happening to the person or group, or do you feel like you do not want to even go beyond the mention of the group name? Do you feel the nation or group is not important to you and your life, perception and value, or do you feel motivated to help, understand, sympathize, or else at the very least learn more about what is happening to that specific group of people, nation or person? That, in essence, is what we are talking about.

Years of study about human nature has taught man a lot. We now know that one can be conditioned to think negative, or even aroused to anger about a group he has never met, known or studied. Such conditioning is based mainly on the bombardment of negative information about the group or nation. You may also be conditioned to love something to the extreme, that you will spend sleepless nights craving for it, after such information bombardment. In the positive sense, for example, carefully crafted commercials are meant to make you love something which otherwise you wouldn't. Companies in the United States literally spend millions a day building an image around a single product they want to market as a fashion trend, be it the Nike shoes, Reebok etc.

A minute of commercial (advertisement) on a carefully chosen television program in the U S, for example, may cost hundreds of thousands of dollars. That is how much people are willing to bet on the efficiency of such tactics. Yes, that is correct, a minute long advertisement. It is no wonder therefore that people get so hooked up and absorbed on such targeted images that young people get sick from hunger in trying to maintain an image of staying slim [an ailment called anorexia], while others take their own lives because they feel they have failed to maintain an image they have set their minds on.

In the negative sense too, people can be driven to extremes by the bombardment of carefully manufactured information, consciously or subconsciously. This statement may need some convincing decades ago, but with today's intense use of negative image building against Muslims in general and Arabs in particular, we do not have to spend a lot of time on this topic. By studying the nature of man, and using such data to manipulate his natural tendencies as a human being, people with sickening mind set have driven mobs to action, citizens to apathy, and intellectuals to sleep.

Today Africa and its nations are struggling to receive their true worth in the eyes of the world. Of all the six inhabited continents on this earth, Africa is the most despised, perceived as the poorest (in terms of real worth in resources, it is not), most disease and poverty prone, and the most expendable. As a result it is the most neglected and usually pushed off and fragmented, in a world that continues to unite and consolidate regionally.

Our world today basically consists of seven continents, six of which humans populate. Africa is the second largest continent on earth, occupying roughly one fifth of its total land area. The Sahara desert takes up one fourth of its total land area, a desert that is also the world's largest. The continent is made up of fifty three (53) countries, all of which are members of the African Union. The regional body has been in existence since 1963, when it was first launched at the dawn of the attainment of self government by many African nations (away from European colonial rule).

Having given our reader the basics about Africa as a continent, and its image in today's world, what then is its true worth? What is Africa made up of? And what is its contribution to the world? These are some of the issues that need to be addressed consistently to weed away the image and self esteem problem so painted, and forcefully maintained. The image and self worth problem in existence today enormously impacts Africans on the continent, and all people of color in the diaspora, who based on race must trace their roots back to Africa. Any attempt therefore to stir any people so affected to positive action, must start with clarifying the true Africa from the image others have painted about it.

The World's Most Enduring Civilization

The world's most enduring civilization on record arose along the Nile River with the most popular and documented section of it being the Delta area that pours into the Mediterranean in present day Egypt. In actual fact however, because Egypt is mostly mentioned by name, people tend to forget that the ancient civilization runs along almost the whole length of the Nile River. And it had at various times within its history that lasted thousands of years beginning at about 3,000 years before Christ (BC), moved capitals upland into areas populated by Abyssinian stock (Ethiopians), Nubians (mostly in Sudan today) and all those nations today that the Nile river passes through them.

Nile is the longest river in the world and runs a course of about 4,000 miles. That is the stretch of such vast civilization. Contemporary historians who tend to see people based on color, class and physique divide the people of that civilization between mainly two stock; the African and Asiatic stock (Mediterranean). Abyssinians and Nubians are some of those categorized under the African stock. Curiously though, with all the bombardment against the African stock as the most backward today, real independent study will lead you to understand that the native Africans were in fact the Kings (Pharaohs) controlling that ancient civilization for most of these years.

In fact if you were to visit the few mummies on display today in museums in Egypt and elsewhere, you will realize the striking resemblance of those mummies to modern day people of African stock, especially the Ethiopians (Abyssinians) and other tall and slim people of East African stock. And the Hamito-Semitic languages found from the Egyptian Delta at the northernmost tip of the continent, which is ancient and includes the languages of the Holy Scriptures (Hebrew included), goes as far inland as West Africa, the Hausa Language of Northern Nigeria being one of them. That is to say that the languages making up the Hamito-Semitic group used to live together thousands of years ago, influencing and impacting each other, and later branching out into various sub sectors and dialects.

In the contemporary image battering of chiefly the European dominated era, Africa found itself being denied its contribution or rightful place as the cradle of mankind, mankind's most dominant and enduring civilization, and one which generated for mankind's development serious study into such subject areas as geometry, astronomy, math, metaphysics, arts, and basically all sciences. Cheikh Anta Diop's study allows us to isolate details of such contributions. It was the African civilization, for example, that was responsible for square roots, balance of quantities, to others as complex as Trigonometry used to calculate the slopes of the pyramids. The Egyptians were also the first in the history of mathematics to pose the problems of the circle's quadrature. In Medicine, seven centuries before Hippocrates, referred to today as the "father of medicine" came into the picture, Dioscorides, Theophrastus and others were describing what they learned from the library of the temple of Imhotep at Memphis. The process of diagnosis and prescription a process used today in medical practice has its roots in African ancient civilization, along the Nile.

After ripping Africa of its contribution, another phase of the negative campaign began, but this time it is mental. That campaign was sought to be necessary, as the lies about black Africans contribution to civilization began to be seriously challenged. The current bastardization of Africa has become so bad, so inherently deliberate that today that part of the world [Egypt and North Africa in general] that was undeniably important in historical development of mankind, has been excised, even if mentally and tagged part of the Middle East; even as we physically see that it is glaringly on the African continent. That is when image destruction to castrate a people becomes a crime, in my humble opinion. When you hear in the news "Sub-Saharan Africa" they are referring to the Nubian or blacker race on the continent, separating them from those of general mixed race of the North African countries of Libya, Algeria, Morocco, Tunisia etc.

Another deliberate action was the disfiguring of the monuments of Egypt. Because the physical monuments of that ancient civilization still stands to this day after thousands of years, people have taken it upon themselves to disfigure some of the markers of the physical characteristics of the statues, so people may not recognize that they have African features. Since the Egyptian Kings will naturally use their own features on such gigantic works and monuments rather than those of foreigners or enemies, the structures became symbols that betray the campaign against the African race. The Sphinx, the figure that has the body of a lion and the head of a human being, has had its nose demolished because it depicts a black person. And if any movie is staged concerning the majesty of the Egyptian civilization today, the characters casted are almost always of the white race (Caucasian).

Most importantly, illusions were implanted into the psyche of everyone but most unfortunately Africans themselves, that they had nothing to do with that civilization and its contribution despite the fact that the Arab invasion (630AD) that brought numerous Arab Middle Easterners into the area until present day did not occur until about three thousand six hundred years after the inception of that civilization (Egyptian first Kingdom).

To be candid, Africans are not denying the Asiatic stock (which the Arabs are categorized into by the same contemporary historians in their illusionary image game) their place in the scheme of things, but authentication of everyone's place serves everyone positively. In his works first appearing 1986 on U S Television as a series and also as a book *"The Africans"*, Professor Ali Mazrui argues that the Arabian

Peninsula, attached to the African continent on its North Eastern region, was regarded as part of the African continent centuries ago, and they intermingled and shared adventures in commerce and knowledge seeking for centuries. Professor Mazrui is an Albert Schweitzer Professor in the Humanities and the Director of the Institute of Global Cultural Studies at the State University of New York, Binghamton. He is of Kenyan origin, born in Mombassa.

Also on the same issue of playing image games to the detriment and bashing of people of African descent, Professor Mazrui highlights the deliberate push by European nations to build the Suez Canal, a calculated attempt to physically separate Africa and its attached Arabian Peninsula or what was later tagged by contemporary European historians as "Middle East" long after the gradual campaign to rename North Africa also, as part of the "Middle East." Since these are calculated actions meant to look innocent, very soon the young generations coming up will never know that the Arabian Peninsula was once attached to the mother continent Africa on its North Eastern border.

That direct connection of the continent to the Arabian Peninsula was what made Prophet Abraham, the patriarch of the three major religions today travel down to Egypt from his place of birth, Ur of Chaldea (in modern day Iraq), after he was persecuted by his people and casted out because of his belief in the One Creator. Just think about what Africa was to many in the world in those days. His people were worshipping carved wood and stones then. People in his situation (scholarly and of contemplative mind) tend to head towards a population for which they would get solace and shelter based on the complexity of what they are talking about, or their ideas. They feel they can get solace in Egypt because even if their idea is brand new, it will not be that much out of place because the level of knowledge and understanding of the people at their intended destination is rich. So if you check the map from Ur of Chaldea to Egypt that was not a long journey.

Another example for my readers is the prophet of Islam. When he was persecuted by his people, the Quraish Arabs, who were worshipping idols principally, he sent his early converts (followers) to Abyssinia (roughly modern day Ethiopia) where the African stock population at that time (about 615AD) were more advanced than their Arab counterparts in religious development. The state religion practiced by King Negus, was Christianity. And to date the orthodox Christianity Ethiopians genuinely inherited from Nabiy Isa Alaihis Salam (Jesus), is alive and well within the Ethiopian midst. That again authenticates the thousands of years of religious development on the African continent, even before the advent of the three scriptural religions in existence today. People were at home with these religions, because their forefathers for thousands of years were on a quest for more physical, mystical and spiritual knowledge anyway, and were becoming better at it with the passage of time.

Abdullahi Yusuf Ali, the most popular translator of the Holy Quran today, in his work "The Meaning of the Quran" has this to say about the significance and central role Egyptian Civilization played in world's historical development, including Islam.

"Of the surviving old civilizations, Egypt and China go back furthest in time with historical material. Egypt has more interest for us, because geographically it was centrally situated, and was influenced by almost every important cultural movement in Asia, Europe, Africa. Nothing happened in Mediterranean history that had not some parts of contact with Egypt." *(Appendix IV, Pg. 404)*

Most people have been conditioned to run away negatively from that civilization and its contribution to world's development because of the famous story of the tyrannical pharaoh that ruled during the Prophethood of Musa (Moses) on him be peace. This negative image, though common across the board, you will find more common among the Muslims. But one has to understand that in a kingdom or civilization especially in dynasties that lasted thousands of years; of course some of the rulers were tyrants and oppressors. But there is no way that all these years, or even most of these years the rulers were a such. The dynasties would not have lasted that long without some sort of credible organization, strong governing structure, and some sort of state policy that supports the community enough to ensure the peace, prosperity and development it enjoyed.

In fact throughout Egyptian history the concept of worship was there, so also life after death as symbolized by the complex burial rituals. Entombed within the Pyramids were many evidences proving the belief in resurrection. Such concepts were developed gradually for thousands of years. In fact, it has been deciphered from Egyptian recorded history that the Pharaoh Amenophis IV (about 1350BC) did adopt the worship of One Supreme God, consequently building a whole new city dedicated to that worship. He called the One God Aton. Imam A.Y. Ali placed the Jewish Prophet Solomon at about "a little after 1000BC", meaning One God worship on the African continent by Amenophis is more than three hundred years earlier than the times of Prophet Solomon.

Abdullahi Yusuf Ali believes more study and appreciation of the contribution of Egyptian knowledge in religious terms is needed as it has generally been neglected in favor of others, such as the ancient Indian religion. In relation to Egyptian civilization he writes:

"Their religious sense was led, in spite of many rebuffs, gradually to a purer conception of man's eternal destiny, until Muhammad's message was preached in the very language in which it was originally preached in Arabia. And that language, Arabic, became and is now the language of the Egyptian people themselves." *(Appendix V, Pg. 408)*

The worship of one God has today become stabilized in Egypt after the Islamic religious influence, and has remained the nation's predominant religion for about one thousand four hundred (1400) years now.

North, East and West African Connections

Tracing the roots and attaching the various African ethnic communities (languages) to their earliest origins is a vast arena, but it has fortunately been documented for thousands of years. Sometimes such facts are etched boldly on rocks and monuments, never to be easily obliterated by destructive image abusers. More recently, anthropology, archeology and the art of linguistics have been very useful in helping piece back together a deliberately dissected communal civilization. It's destroyed and mostly disfigured relics which developed the intricate artistic, scientific, and religious knowledge over many centuries, and actually thousands of years, have been recovered by its sons and daughters long after the event.

Most recently, the same destructive elements who are not really interested in a just and harmonious world, have out of vested interest, for example, caused a chaotic situation between some of the most respected intellectual authorities living among us today, who might have helped us further in such quests. When Professor Ali Mazrui uncovered and introduced these dichotomies, filling in the details of hard truths about what Africa was and is (back in 1986), and what its population has offered and continues to offer the world, another Professor was sponsored out of Harvard University to counter some of those hard truths in 1999 by virtually the same sponsors, the Corporation for Public Broadcasting with his series *Wonders of the African World* which premiered October 25-27, 1999. That Professor is Henry Louis Gates. But for African greater interest, this is not necessary, and is actually counterproductive. It is a ploy, in my opinion, to make sure the Africans on the continent, and those in the Diaspora do not join together for any common good.

My opinion is, the sponsors used, most importantly among other possible factors, the difference in religion between the two to cause that discord. Professor Henry Louis Gates is a Christian African American, while Professor Ali Mazrui is a Muslim born on the continent of Africa (Mombasa, Kenya), but has resided for many of his productive years in the U.S. as a Professor. That deliberate friction created between the two- one going out to counter the other later- is not necessary as the facts they set their minds to bring out are of common importance to them both and their individual regional communities, plus all three Abrahamaic faiths. I will give you a typical example. As an undergraduate student on the continent of Africa during the acquisition of this writer's first degree (Mass Communication), this writer studied along the way, African History. Though casually introduced to such issues (because her degree specialization was in communication), she was blind to some of those basic connective facts until she took up a job as an International Radio Broadcaster.

While we broadcast in Hausa (a widely spoken West African language concentrated in Nigeria), my Ethiopian neighbors did in Amharic, both of which are brother languages from ancient Hamito-Semitic languages of all three scriptures. Because we have common internal radio monitors direct from the studios of broadcasts, while listening to their language I will walk over to them and say you have many Hausa words in your language, what does such and such mean in your language? They will tell me. Most of the time, it does not directly mean the same thing, owing to the fact that the connection between the two languages was from thousands of years, but the meaning is not completely off. Mostly the meaning within both languages is still within a general context, i.e. the general subject area within which the word was used.

A broadcasting colleague at that time named Yeheyes Wuhib (Christian), with a collaborated name with my son Yahaya Wada (Muslim), both first names going back to the same root word, once mentioned in a discussion that the idea that Aramaic, the language Isa (Jesus) on him be peace spoke is almost lost (as most contemporary image destructive historians say is not a living language today), is not true. Amharic, his language is believed by his people to be closely related to Aramaic (the language Jesus preached in). But here is the point most people miss, causing most of us to allow ourselves to be manipulated by image destructors into barking at each other, tearing each other down, or else doing the extreme, picking weapons to fight and kill each other. It is just not necessary.

Both languages of Hausa and Amharic have thousands of year's connections beyond the three Abrahamaic scriptures (Hebrew, Aramaic and Arabic). It is a result of myopic and narrow mindedness that the adherents of the two religions that came through two brother languages on the continent and abroad might think their world is that different, enough to lunge at each other at any time down the line as history continues to unfold. In short ancient Hebrew (Biblical Hebrew), Aramaic, and Arabic have common ancestral connections with the speakers of Hausa and Amharic. So one wonders as to what the two intellectuals with roots in the African civilization were fighting about? And what are we today as a people who follow the religions of our common ancestors fighting about?

Coming back to our common language awakening I had in those years, I remember well when a broadcaster by the name of Girma was first introduced at the Ethiopian languages section, I walked over to him, naturally curious all the time about such connections across the continent; I told him your name means something in my language. Girma is an adjective, sometimes used as a noun to denote status. It is aligned to post, position etc sometimes used as a "post." and sometimes "position." Later down the road I learnt today the Ethiopian President is named Girma.

That is only a connection with another Hamito-Semitic language. In actual fact however, the Hamito-Semitic languages have been further classified into six branches, each branch more connected with each other within their group than the other five groups. Incidentally, Hausa as a language, the Chadic branch, appears to have more direct and close connection with the Ancient Egyptian language (at the Delta region of modern day Egypt) than many others so classified. The other five groups apart from Chadic are Egyptian, Cushite, Berber, Omotic and Semitic.

If you intend to study further I would advice that you watch out for a more recent attempt to excise the darker skinned language speakers from the groups. This movement began in early 1900s. The newer generation advocates of excising the darker races from the ancient group term the classification Afro-asiatic, instead of Hamito-Semitic. Hamito-Semitic is however still more acceptable in academic circles, than the newer theories.

With that process through language connections also, I have had my own personal reflections. In the field of Linguistics, language connections, and the route of dispersion (migration) of various groups are traced based on the percentage of shared vocabularies. And in tracing what language is more ancient and which is an offshoot of which the technique involves sharing basic root words that describe the simplest form of existence in prehistoric eras. For example words that describes water, fire, hunting, etc.

Personal Encounter with that Connection

In the writers reflections based on such arts, she came to a realization of the direct religious connections with Early Egyptian civilizations from the word "Ra" for example, that describes a deity worshipped thousands of years ago in dynastic era Egypt. Amun Ra is a Sun god, in Egyptian mythology, who was actually supposed to be a higher god to whom the other lesser gods serve under, him being the head. In Hausa language the celestial Sun is called "Rana." Ra can stand on its own as a word within Hausa syntax with "Rana" making it a possessive noun meaning "My Ra." (My Sun) endearing it to self. In linguistic analysis, that factual connection, along with other factors, may denote sun worship, the worship of Ra along with the Egyptians at some time in the past. This has indeed been substantiated by other relevant data. That further connects the Hausa with biblical Queen of Sheba, who became the wife of Biblical Solomon, and whose people were sun worshippers from Abyssinia. One need to understand that though Sun worship is very common, the worship of Amon Ra, tagged the King of the gods of Egypt was the only one we know in History named as such. And he ruled both the Upper and Lower Egypt consisting of both Egypt and Abyssinia at about 1600BC.

Listening once to a former Nigerian Ambassador to the United Nations Alhaji Yusuf Maitama Sule speak at this writer's college campus in Nigeria during "Hausa Week" it further vindicates the writer's quest. In an annual event to study and further enrich the cultural heritage of its speakers, Alhaji Maitama (speaking at the occasion) was recounting that he could remember a legendary song from childhood passed down for generations that denotes to him some sort of sun worship thousands of years back by the Hausa people. He also in his lecture at the event, argued credibly about that connection with Abyssinians. The song goes like this *"Rana, rana fito fito in yanka miki ragon baba ki sha jini tsar tsar."* The literal translation is **The Sun please rise, and I will sacrifice for you my father's ram."**

So in short, the Hausa community who are predominantly Muslim by religion today, with about eighty percent of them living in Nigeria (at least ninety five percent of those and above Muslim), and also existing in lesser numbers in many countries of West Africa have in their ancestral past been part and parcel of an ancient civilization that strove in the quest for artistic, scientific, and religious knowledge which consequently culminated in all three scriptural religions (Jewish, Christian and Muslim) as practiced today on the face of the earth. It appears that the Hausa ancestors have gone through all such religious eras spanning thousands of years, each time accepting the higher knowledge that makes sense to them, as it evolves, and incorporating it in their lives, to arrive at the present day Muslim Hausa. The Hausas are an honorable people, honored by their contribution to a great civilization dating back thousands of years, and honored by God by being part of a greater nation of people through which His three scriptural revelations were delivered to mankind.

They also have an ancestral connection to the people that made it possible today to manufacture and develop all these technological inventions in science, medicine, technology etc. It is time for them, we believe, to rediscover their rich ancestral past, and rise above the destructive mechanizations of image destroyers working under the grip of the evil one, aiming to throw their people and land into perpetual chaos and bloodshed. It is possible that God still has some hope in them, but they have to rise up and do the right thing.

Since 1999, the Hausa have been primarily at the receiving end of what appears to be a grand design to make them victims of mass negative image campaign. With the global targeting of Muslims, and the Hausa being an ethnic group with the largest percentage of Muslims in Nigeria, specific groups in the country choose to kill them at will, whenever they feel like it. A positive sense of self worth, or what today may be termed image repair and contribution acknowledgment, will go a long way in raising the determination of the Hausa people to self-defense and reclaiming of their enduring heritage which may ultimately help the whole country.

So Nigerians as a nation have a sizable population tracing the same roots with the greatest and most enduring civilization in world history. The West Africans also have among them one of the biggest groups, the Fula or Fulani who stretch from Futa Toro in the Sene Gambian region, all the way to the East African border countries of Cameroon Chad etc with their life chiefly revolving around cattle herding. Their movement year long in search of pasture, something they have done also for thousands of years have spread them across the whole region. West Africans of the Sene Gambian regions at the westernmost tip of the continent were believed to have set out on Ocean explorations thousands of years back. Some sources believe they may be part of a people that reached the coast of South America and North America long before the European expeditions that brought Columbus, for example. River Niger, the third longest river on the continent of Africa stretching across the region for 2600 miles starts from the mountain range of Gambia, crossing the region into the Western part of Nigeria, then pours out to the Atlantic ocean in the delta region of Southern Nigeria.

Many sources and scholarly studies conducted; among them Ivan Gladstone Van Sertima, in his book, "They Came before Columbus" published in 1976 argue that Africans were engaged in explorations and expeditions by sea centuries ago. In the Book, Sertima, an honor graduate of University of London who went to the School of Oriental and African Studies in 1959, argued based on archeological facts that Africans were in contact with Central and South American sub continent, impacting their lives and cultures long before the era of Christopher Columbus who is generally believed today, to be the first expedition to "discover" the American continent. The drawings and figurines excavated, with their corresponding carbon dating data shows, and further authenticate the extent and depth of West African scientific and exploratory knowledge at that time, which enabled them to undertake such expeditions.

If you want to gain and understand the standpoint of Van Sertima and his works especially where he argued the scientific contribution of Africans to the world, you may want to read a collection of his works from 1999 titled *African Renaissance*. He credibly argued his conclusions. But as we have already impressed on you, there are many who work tirelessly against such efforts, believing their race's rise and hold on power and resources depend on putting other races down.

Van Sertima's work had its share of critics. A critic by the name of Glyn Daniel wrote *The New York Times* discrediting the works of Van Sertima as "ignorant rubbish." In response another scholar of Archeology who had spent a significant portion of his life, about forty years, studying the same South American culture, Clarence Weiant, came to Sertima's defense. Weiant, contacted the New York Times in writing, arguing that Ivan Sertima has spent years of meticulous research and his conclusions were "based upon Archeology, Egyptology, African History, Oceanography, Astronomy, Botany, rare Arabic and Chinese manuscripts, the letters and journals of early American explorers and the observations of physical anthropologists." Clarence Weiant further states that "I am thoroughly convinced of the soundness of Van Sertima's conclusions."

Contributions of Van Sertima and other scholars

Van Sertima was not the first to introduce those facts to the world using the most convincing proofs, which portray how so early African explorers, merchants and even religious figures sailed across the Ocean to what today is known as South America. In the introductory past of his book, for example, he introduced readers to earlier works by two scholars, German-Americans, one a Harvard Linguist named Leo Wiener and a Professor Alexander Von Wuthenau. Apart from archives he studied, Prof Wuthenau, an archeologist, had practically unearthed "a large number of Negroid heads in clay, gold, copper and copal sculpted by pre-Columbian American artists." That is not the only shocking news, but the era these excavations go back to is amazing. The strata (layer of earth) where they were found range from the earliest Native American civilizations up to and beyond Columbus contact with the region. The two scholars influenced the quest of Van Sertima and stirred his interest. But it was Ivan van Sertima that literally illuminated the world with that part of history.

From archives of Columbus (journal entries) and writings about his expeditions it was discerned that Columbus sailed with six ships "set for the exploration of the route the African Marines had taken to the New World." Guinean and the Sierra Leonean areas were at that time quoted as having some unique spears that have on its tip an alloy of metals never seen before. (See also Leo Wiener, in *Africa and the Discovery of the Americas*; Philadelphia, Innes and Sons, 1920-1922, Vol. 1) Captivated by such convincing evidence, Professor Wuthenau writes "It is in contradiction to the most elementary logic and all artistic experience that an Indian could depict in a masterly way the head of a Negro without missing a single racial characteristic, unless he had actually seen such a person."

More recently in history is the story of an African King Abubakar II setting out in 1311 with some large boats filled with food and provisions across the Atlantic. This incident, occurring some 700 years ago, has also been documented in both Mali and Cairo. He embarked from the

Sene-Gambian Coast, and two of the ships were reported to have returned with stories about the Mexican people. Earlier excavations in Mexico about the presence of Africans date from just before Christ to periods after Christ.

The Negroid features of the pre-Columbian excavations were so convincing that even critics find it hard to deny African contact predating Columbus who for long was associated with being the first to set foot on American sub continent from other parts of the world already discovered. Soon however some were arguing that these Africans could not be independent rich merchants or affluent traders, but servants. But that premise has been shattered by many credible signs of the influence of these early explorers.

Some of the proofs of their status could be discerned from some archeological findings too. For example, it is believed that the Africans brought some of their advanced religious concepts and orders along with them. Some African Statues and figurines, like the ones found among a people called the Olmes, stood at between 6-9 feet high at special temples. They appear to be early primitive gods worshipped among the Olmes. The shrines were located in La Venta, about 18 miles from the coast of Gulf of Mexico.

It has been also documented from archeological artifacts and other recorded data that the Mandingos of West Africa traded with the Mexicans. They bought from Africa brightly colored clothes which the native people described as beautiful like the feathers of the birds. Also among items traded were plumages, and animal skins. Other evidences of religious connections between the two include relics and terms. In Mandingo culture, for example, there is a cult of the werewolf called *nama*, and its head or priest is called *tigi*. The two words are put together in their local vocabulary as *nama-tigi*, which has been found among the Mexicans too. The ritual in Mexico includes the wearing of wolf skin and is called *aman teca*.

Other writers such as Jan Carew in his book *"African Presence in the Americas"* sought to clarify some issues about the difference responsible for the ignorance of many to the African early influence on South America. The difference lies in the manner of contact with the Americas and Columbus's. Carew described the first natives of the Americas that came into contact with Columbus as the Indians of the Lucayo tribe living in Guanahini. The people told Columbus and his crew that earlier explorers by sea have informed them of a hairy people who wore beard before, but they had never seen them until Columbus contact.

Carew argued that, just because Columbus, a European from Spain with a different psyche and mindset of conquest, operating mostly through looting riches and grabbing lands he lands on by force in the name of his foreign aristocracy, it does not mean that for all these years other people with a more friendly contact have not set foot on the American continent.

A museum in Mexico named after Alexander von Wuthenau to date attracts multitudes of scholars of African History, especially those interested in ancient pre-Columbian presence of African influence in the Americas. A scholar of history from the Caribbean, Tiho Narva, visiting the museum for the first time wrote "How could we have ignored such overwhelming evidence for so long!"

It is still unbelievable to many. Van Sertima wrote regarding the large African statues in the temples of the Americas: "It is hard for many to imagine the Negro-African figure being venerated as a god among the American Indians. He has always been represented as the lowest of the low, at least since the era of conquest and slavery."

Debunking Religious Stigmatization

All three Semitic and scriptural religions whose followers believe the founders spoke God's words to their followers, have strong roots in Africa. They are not imports, as many believe, but they are offshoots of a continent that has for thousands of years been in a quest for a sense of higher power. It started thousands of years ago, along the Nile that natured the first ancient human that walked the earth, four million years ago in the valleys along the Nile. That was how far back the carbon dating placed the archeological remains of the most ancient humanoid to be found to date. No intellectual today worth his professional name will doubt that Africa indeed is the cradle of mankind. The humanoid remains were found in the valleys of Ethiopia. The same area where it is believed today, that man first walked the earth as a human. And Ethiopia is just one of the communities of the Nile civilization.

How then, did religion begin among such a people of early civilization? How did the oldest civilization bore the idea of appeasing a greater power? It all started with a sense of limit to the power of man to control all his essential needs. For example, where does the power controlling the floods of the Nile reside? For its stability is important for the irrigation of the rich lands that border it. Where does the power controlling the fertility of the soil reside? For it is important for bountiful harvest. And by the way where does the power behind unceasing rain in the spring reside, for it provides the grass for pasture.

The answers were thought to lie in the forces of rain, forces of the rivers and those of the sky and earth. Man began to worship and make appeasing offerings to those forces. Later as the kingdom developed, still with similar idea of appeasing the one that controls man's development and material survival, the Kings became the lords.

Meanwhile however, serious study into those forces and their influence on man continues. The reason being that, it was not mainly based on material needs that these forces were being appeased, but for curiosity too. The persistent quest to answer greater questions that beset man's mind, a natural inquisitiveness led a people to continue to seek knowledge. Man's nature is always geared towards learning the truths behind every action, object or even the transient speech. Truths lead to acceptance and endearment. It brings peace into a mind and heart that was not long ago filled with doubts and uncertainty. For that the quests continued. It led to ancient sun dials, temples, dams and pyramids. It led to construction of structures that defy the weathering of environmental elements for thousands of years, and defied the know how of the arrogant technological braggarts of today, for none of them today, could replicate the technique used to erect such massive structures.

The idea today that Islam is a problem on the African continent is part of the image destructive agenda. It grew over the years. But Islam was not introduced by force to Africans, but through commercial and cultural interactions that came chiefly with intercontinental trade. That was what made Islam relevant and adaptable to the continent. Over thousands of years, many cultural influences came and went, and the impact they had depended upon its adaptability, and value. The Greeks and the Romans, the Turks and the Persians all had their days. Either by explorations, war and conquest, or for spread of ideas they came and went. Some made great impact, some moderate and some almost none, when talking about incorporation of their ideas and ways into the daily lives on an average African.

Many of the continent's Islamic ideas like allowance for more than one wife if one chooses to, discipline and timeliness in worship daily, the special attention to building the spiritual part of man rather than emphasis on materialism are some of the values that were easily adaptable to a continent natured for long along most of these basic life values. Some of the values that were common continent wide before Islamic influence include hospitality, so also the concept of family not stopping at the husband wife and children, but incorporating the grandparents, uncles and aunts, nephews and nieces, commonly termed as extended family.

Women were not only freer in African ancient culture, they were generally independent to a great degree to choose a profession, who to marry and have greater control of their life limitations in terms of hard work and contribution to family and community. There were the Queens and the warriors, like Queens Bilkis (Abyssinia 1000 BC), Nzinga (Angola 1583-1663 AD), Nefertiti (1370-1330BC, Egypt), Queen Tiye also, the mother of Akhnaton and mother in law of Nefertiti, Cleopatra (69 – 30BC, Egypt) and Hashepsut (1508 – 1458 BC, Egypt), Amina (1536-1583 AD, Nigeria) etc. They all led not just the political decisions, but military decisions and diplomacy. They led their people to battlefields too. Women in Ghanaian communities, even to date, regardless of religious background or language differences generally are freer than in most nations especially in commerce. Ask Ghanaians today about the Kalabule, and they will tell you a lot.

In earlier African agrarian culture, the concept of polygamy especially in rural communities was widespread. That allowed men the children they needed as farmhands. Furthermore in African culture before then, you never hog material, or lock your door to your kin just because sharing will reduce the material comfort of your immediate primary family. The bonds of love and companionship transcend the barrier of greed, and material possession.

The extended families of grandparents were cherished as the possessors of wisdom. That used to be where you go when life becomes challenging, to gain wisdom from the sea of experience, and knowledge from the past. It was not only respect that was accorded the old, the young feel blessed to care for them. No one in a typical African setting went hungry, even if he grew old alone, with no children or spouse to care for him or her. The daily subsistence of such people was the responsibility of their kin and neighbors.

Even those who had no children, or else those mad and handicapped, got their daily food from their neighbors. Everyone was part of his community. In fact as the historians will tell you, because of this bond many African languages do not have specific words for cousins, nephews and nieces, because your sister's or brother's children are automatically your children, so you treat as well as address them like your own biological children.

All these inherent cultural values made Islam adaptable in many ways. We say in many ways because it was not a perfect match however. Though not the worst of its practitioners in the world and definitely not the first; slavery had left a stigma for Arabs. That stigma extends beyond its cultural value into the realms of the religion of Islam. But to be fair to the religion, it is an established cultural phenomenon. Restrictive values for women was also alien to ancient African culture, and to date even after the influence of Arab culture, Muslim women on the continent are generally freer that those in Arab countries. Most ancient African communities have strong matrilineal influence, while Arab culture is patrilineal. For further studies on this subject of women status in ancient African culture, you may want to read the writings of Cheikh Anta Diop and others.

But to be fair to the Arabs or as is sometimes used synonymously Islam, slavery predates the propagation of Islam and the popularity of Arab culture. Since the father of all three scriptural religions, Patriarch Abraham, the Old Testament is full of examples of noble families who own and give out slaves. These accounts about the Hebrew Prophets came down to us through Jewish Scholars. Slaves were gifted by wives to their husbands as in some versions of the story of Hagar, the ancestral mother of the Arabs, who they say was gifted to Sarah from the palace of the King of Egypt. Some other sources say she was a noble from the palace, not a slave. But even the Prophet Jacob (Israel) was related to have had sons with two slaves who were gifted to him as consorts by his two wives Leah and Rachel, who own the two slaves.

To conclude therefore, history has not done justice to Africans. Not only did it deny Africans their birthright, it went to great lengths to hide and obliterate all positive influences of African knowledge and contributions to global development. Their legacy was in short stolen from them, and painted Caucasian and "white." Pharaohs and rich Egyptian nobles are today depicted as people of white skin and European physique. And it was not until about mid last century 1900s, when Africans on the continent and also in the diaspora, especially United States began a more credible fight to free themselves from physical and psychological domination. It was from that era onwards that serious studies and books began to emerge in larger numbers challenging such lies and deceptions.

The Color Question

Africans on the continent may not be the most pressed to know the dynamics of the ongoing color war in the world. The colonial experience after all, has just "physically" ended some half century in the past. Though that should not have made people sit back, we can generally say that the African struggle for progress and equal treatment as any other human or nations of this planet has not generally been effective yet.

But the African American, who has to some degree made progress in raising his status from that of less than a human to a full human being at about the same time as the African struggling to free himself from colonial control, half a century ago, is still engaged in that struggle today. For that reason, we will look into what he has discovered. He lives among the most developed of the European societies on this planet, and has a first hand experience of the color battle. He might not have chosen that fight, but for his survival he has been forced to carry on with it.

First of all, one has to understand that genetically, Africans have the capacity within their genes to produce people or various hues, from their own color at one extreme, to a completely white human, and all other colors in between. This is an accepted genetically confirmed phenomenon. The first human to walk the earth, as far as we know today, is an African from the continent. If you live on the African continent, you might have seen how two fully black African couple came together to give birth to the most light skinned individual (Albino), a genetic deficiency of a chemical known as melanin that gives skin its dark tone. Recent progress in genetics that made it possible to map the complete human genome (or genetic code), has confirmed that you can get all the races on this planet from an African.

People of the "white" race, popularly called Europeans or Caucasians however, cannot produce people of other colors by themselves. They can only produce their own color. They are not in the majority either. Three quarters of the world population belong to people of various hues, from black, to brown, yellow and red and all colors in between. It is for that reason, according to a popular psychologist who had written numerous papers on this phenomena, Dr. Francis Cress Welsing, that people of European origin classifying themselves as "white" assume a mindset that they are in danger of being wiped out as a race, and in essence punishing every other race on the planet for something creative from day one, for which they have no part in determining.

The genetic make up of a human being is not a subjective issue that man has anything to do with, or ability that he has determined by himself. Genetics came intact from God the Creator of humans, and the impact of people of color being stronger than that of the white race along with it. The reality is that all other races except the white race can produce people with a degree of shade of darker skin, or some form of color. Which according to psychologists mean that the odd race of all the others is the white race. By this they mean it is a deficiency that one would assume they would accept and mingle with everyone else as is done by everyone, not choose to punish everyone because their race is the only one that have the inability to produce children of color.

The whole world however is being made to accommodate that mind set of white supremacy. It has permeated all aspects of life, social, economic, political, commercial and all else across the world. All people who objectively studied racism and its effect on the world advocate a social campaign that will change that course of action in order to reach and maintain a peaceful and just world. Though not directly attacking that system as such, many white race individuals have also reached the conclusion that the present world system needs to be overturned for a more just and fair system that will bring some semblance of development, eradicating the seething poverty and injustice to majority of the world population. But to do that effectively, one needs a deeper understanding of the mind set, the process, and the structure of racism across the world. The Color-Confrontation Theory presented by Dr Welsing in her 1991 book *The Isis Papers* is a good start.

So what is racism, and is it confined only to the United States where it is mostly used and practiced? In his 1969 publication, Neely Fuller explains that "racism is not only a pattern of individual and/or institutional practice; it is a universally operating 'system' of white supremacy and domination in which the majority of the world's white people participate" [Welsing, 1991]. Going further on this same premise, Dr. Welsing argued credibly about the why, how, and the what, sector of the phenomena. Briefly she sees it as emanating from inadequacy turned on its head to make the adequate majority (with abilities to produce color) feel inferior, and in the process designing a self-serving system that keeps the race "pure," their pockets full, and their power and domination in place.

She however seem to think that, as a psychological phenomenon, the white race could be helped by world psychologists who have seriously conducted studies about racism, such as herself, if the white supremacists are genuinely looking for ways to accept their situation that is not manmade, and embrace a more community based thinking, co-existence on the one habitable planet on our solar system. She writes:

"...white people of the world presumably also could benefit from such an awareness of the motivation behind behaviors that often baffle them. If they are sincere in their attempts to stop the practices of white supremacy (racism), whites may be able to find methods to do so once the cause is understood." (Welsing, 1991 Pg. 13)

Effect of Racism on World History

The seriousness of this color war has forced contemporary historians to write history as it best fits them, away from reality, so much so that one has to go on a quest with an open mind to find real and more credible history from fragments and put it together.

A typical example of such findings shows that the earliest people that occupied Chaldea, where the father of the three Godly faiths came from are Black Africans generally known far back in history as Kushites (from Kush, or Cush). An English Orientalist by the name of General Sir Henry Rawlinson, after an intense archeological and philological study concluded that the dominant race in Babylonia at the earliest time to which the monuments reached back in history was Kush. And he is not the only one, or even the first to reach that conclusion.

People classified as Kushites have black African (negroid) features. Most closely referred to that group today are Abyssinians (Ethiopians). Ethiopian as a term was used as a general term in the ancient times for black skinned people. Just as the Egyptians civilization has today been contracted to stereo-typify modern day Egypt within its border, whereas it spanned the whole length of the Nile River, Ethiopia was a name first given the black race by the Greek, and later used generally for the race by Historians and others. Kushites and Hamites are sometimes interchangeably used also. It should be noted that Hamites as a term has its roots in one individual Ham. Ham is one of the children of Noah. The descendants of Ham are Hamites. Whenever they are classified as a group they are generally meant to denote people of black African ancestry or characteristics.

Also for those who study the Old Testament, the oldest of the three religious scriptures of the Abrahamaic faith, they will find that the genealogy of the sons of Ham (Tenth chapter of Genesis) derives Nimrod from Kush, not Kush from Nimrod. Nimrod is celebrated as a Mesopotamian Monarch. If we go by the Torah then, Hamites from Africa migrated eastward to populate what today is termed the Arabian Peninsula, and the Euphrates. In Genesis we learn the genealogy of Ham. Accordingly his sons were Kush, Mizraim, Phut, and Cannan, and Kush begat Nimrod.

Ham is a son of Noah and Ham is the father of Nimrod, and in some versions the grandfather of Nimrod. Nimrod, a Mesopotamian Monarch was one of the most famous founders of the kingdoms that developed in the Mesopotamian region, associated with building several cities, and with commissioning the construction of the Tower of Babel. Mesopotamia is the region or civilization that evolved around the two rivers Tigris and Euphrates, now in modern day Iraq. The story of that tower though contradicts Godly worship for which Noah and his progeny were known. Though some sources in Hebrew and later Arabic brings Nimrod to a physical encounter with Biblical Abraham, portraying him as a paganistic king, the Bible did not mention that. In Biblical genealogy, Abraham did not arrive on the scene until ten generations after Noah.

It may be worthwhile at this juncture to set some facts straight for greater understanding of what follows. As described by John G. Jackson an authority in Ancient African studies in his introduction to Lane-Poole, Stanley's book "The Story of the Moors in Spain," in ancient times, Black Africans were generally referred to as Ethiopians; in medieval times Africans were called Moors; and in modern times Africans were called Negroes. Ethiopians in short meant "burnt face' and were given that name by the Greeks when they first come in contact with them. *Ethios* meant burnt in the language of the Greek.

According to Jackson "The word Negro was manufactured during the Atlantic Slave Trade to categorize a group of people. To put it another way, there are many species of small fish in the ocean; when put into cans they are called sardines. There are no free fish called sardines." Jackson further explained that the derogatory term came only after such Africans became enslaved and put in chains, just as a fish only became a sardine when canned.

We may assume that racism took a new turn after the decision to buy and sell Africans as commodities during the third modern era that named the Africans carried away in that manner as negroes. In fact Jackson says the Hamites, Ethiopians and Moors are viewed as the Progressive Africans. Others are viewed as the backward ones and termed Negro. Trans-Atlantic slave trade evolved the term Negroes.

And finally, Arabia and Spain. For the Arabian Peninsula once again we may be able to make a more concise presentation by quoting a former Prime Minister to the Sultan of Muscat, Oman Dr. Bertram Thomas who noted:

"The original inhabitants of Arabia...were not the familiar Arabs of our own time, but a very much darker people. A protonnegroid belt of mankind stretched across the ancient world from Africa to Malaya. This belt by environmental and other evolutionary processes became in parts transformed, giving rise to the Hamitic people of Africa to the Dravidian peoples of India, to an intermediate dark people inhabiting the Arabian Peninsula. In the course of time two big migrations of fair skinned peoples came from the north ...the Mongoloids...and the other the Caucasoid to drive a wedge between India and Africa." (Dr. Thomas)

And much closer to recent history, colored people from North African region crossed the Mediterranean into Spain, captured it and ruled for seven hundred years. They were a mixture of Moors and Berbers, who were part of the army of a great general of that time named Tarek. They brought to that part of Europe knowledge, development and architectural beauty as was not seen earlier in the land. They were known as Moors of North Africa. Before they entered Spain, under the direction of an Islamic governor of North Africa Musa Ibn Noseyr, the country has been ruled for two hundred years by people known as the Visigoths (West Goths), a less civilized people historians called "barbarians" who took advantage of the decline of the Roman empire to attack and occupy some vestiges of Rome.

Under the command of Tarek the Moor, a Moor army of about 7,000 was said to have set out camping at Gebal Tarek (Gibraltar) then moving on to attack. Though the governor, Musa was sent by Khalifa Waled from Arabia, the North Africa he oversees was made up of Berbers and Moors. These groups of colored Africans conquered and ruled Spain for seven centuries. Though some sources tend to show or give the impression that the people then looked like modern day lighter Arab, the Moors were in actual fact a brown and dark skinned people of North Africa at that time.

Chapter Two

Nigerian Economic Challenges

Defining Some of the Most Urgent Socio-Economic Problems of Nigeria

This was a paper first delivered at a conference on Socio-Economic Development of Nigeria in Leeds, United Kingdom in August of 2008. The Conference was organized by the Nigerian Muslim Forum UK.

Introduction

Today, I intend to do what people generally do not do. I just pray that you have the patience to follow me with an open mind. I intend to talk from both sides of my brain and my inner conscience, to address the problem at hand. By that I mean, the creative and devine, the academics and theology. I believe, to be sincere to ourselves and at the same time effectively ponder the problems, we have to address the issues from both parts that made us who we are as a creation, the body and the soul, the physical and the spiritual.

One of our main problems today, and this is global by the way, is we have been so carried away by the academic, scientific and technological developments of our times, as if in and of themselves they can free us from our daunting problems. We use knowledge in utter disregard of what is ethically and morally right. Instead of creatively applying such knowledge to solve problems, we get carried away by it.

The ethical and moral question are the domain of spiritual development, and the devine orders. And the world today has forcefully been made to tread the secular path primarily, leaving the sacred part that deals with spiritual development to the temples, churches and mosques. But if we want to look at ourselves comprehensively, we have no choice but to access both parts of us in this journey. The development of these two aspects helps to counterbalance our conduct as beings made up of a soul and a body.

Institutions, science and technology are tools for the use of man towards creating positive implements, and directing their uses towards positive goals. Man is supposed to be the master of those tools. Furthermore, with the right intention, through that application of knowledge in resolving his fellow human's problems, he gains a reward that keeps reproducing itself (*Sadaqatul Jariyah*), blessings (*Barakah*) in his wealth, and probably professional development in the likes of promotions and recognitions if he is interested in that.

But that is not the general direction the application of such knowledge today takes. We have in existence today, a 'disconnect' situation between knowledge and its application for "true advancement" because such tools have been misused. I will give you a typical example. Nuclear energy could be used to supply uninterrupted electricity to millions for rapid socio-economic development; while at the same time it could be used to produce weapons of mass destruction to annihilate people; but unfortunately the world has preferred to mostly put it into use for the latter.

Satellites could be positively used to pry our globe for better production of food, water supply, location of natural resources including how much is available underground for effective planning, use and distribution. These services have the potential to eliminate hunger, diseases, neutralize tensions between nations up in struggle for control of meager resources, and provide alternatives for better use of such resources. But it can also be used to spy on nations providing spy reports and distributing it to nations of the world to start wars, and escalate those already in progress. The world has chosen the latter in most cases. A major reason for creating and escalating such wars, by the way, is to create market for the weapons industries of the industrialized world.

I hope you will forgive me then, if I venture off the normal track that conferences such as this usually dwell on, and pry into what I believe are our most serious problems. While doing so, we will try to asses them, and provide some recommendations.

The Premise

Every nation has its unique set of prospects and problems. Nigeria is one of them. In order to address them effectively, we have to originate our own research, diagnostics, experiment with applicable solutions on a sample level, and then choose the most effective means of dealing with it. We must have the courage to implement those solutions no matter how bitter it may taste, or hard it may feel in the short term. If we truly want change to usher in prosperity and development on a mass level, we have to realize it may not be easy.

Many professionals, agencies and well intentioned citizens, have attempted what we are doing here today, but the problems remain. What then is the hindrance? Some of the major reasons behind the failure to make any impact in that direction could be categorized into three major areas (a) The commitment to solving the problems was lacking (b) those in whose hand the resources of the nation are, who enjoy the status quo, may not be willing to commit it to workable solutions that may ultimately shake that status quo; (c) and even if they do, those entrusted to implement the promising and well thought out recommendations, fall into the same past practices they were entrusted with funds to eradicate. The question then is: Do we have hope that Nigeria can really find its way back to solid ground?

It is not impossible, because we have seen countries that were like Nigeria years ago, revolutionalized their attitude towards nation building and community development and made great strides. Today they have become a force to reckon with worldwide. Nations of Asia are an example, such as Japan, and in most recent times, China, Malaysia, and Indonesia. The situation for Nigeria then is; are Nigerians and their government willing to; (a) commit to the solutions (b) ultimately sweat it through.

I assure you all that it will not be easy. Ask management professionals who have been working continually on designing and implementing changes in their organizations, a simpler entity, compared to a complex society like Nigeria. But as I say, it is NOT impossible and actually I am optimistic that with the right government dedicated to the good of all, we can launch and sustain such an undertaking, and make the most of it.

Hindrances to socio-economic development in the case of Nigeria

The Nigerian governing and administrative system has been handicapped by many problems. They are not insurmountable however. But because they have been so much entrenched it will take a mass campaign for an attitude change and a commitment from the people and their government to eradicate it. This is because as heinous and as reprehensible as these problems are, they have gradually become acceptable practices. And mind you, they have become acceptable practices not because people do not have what we call in Islam *Fitra*, the inborn compass designed by our Creator to point us towards Him, and thereby internally alert us about the wrong and the right way (of God's universal law).

So, because people chose to ignore that compass by forcefully neglecting it and violating God's law, they gradually reprogrammed their Fitra to their personal desires; what we may call in Islamic terms "they have wronged their own souls. Souls, we must understand, are separate entities entrusted to us during our material life on the earth. So what people collectively do today with their deliberately misguided values has contributed greatly to the abysmal condition we find ourselves today as a nation. People who ignore and violate their inborn compass end up cheating themselves and jeopardizing others. With repeated violations, very soon they have formed a behavioral pattern hard to move away from. In Nigeria, it does not stop there however.

As people corrupt themselves and their souls; they force such practices onto others, including their subordinates, and ordinary Nigerians too. This is precisely where the adage that the best among the people in moral and ethical values should lead comes from. And that appointing a corrupt leader spreads corruption in the whole land. A leader in every sense of the word is the person who gives directions as to what is to be done to his immediate staffs, who then pass it on down the ranks to those holding the lowest ranks. But what if the leader is a corrupt individual, with a corrupted soul, which ultimately gives him corrupted directives?

The subordinate is forced into a choice of either implementing his superior's corrupt and ethically bankrupt practices on others, or being shown the door to unemployment. For clarity, moral issues are those that relate to a person's personal character and behavior the ultimate source of guidance for it being divine orders from which his religious bearing emanates. Ethical issues on the other hand relate to his professional conduct, i.e. the laws of righteousness that enhances his job such as "saving lives' for Doctors and "social responsibility" for the press (journalists). As experience shows over the years, a vast majority of subordinates will not make the right choice between following corrupt directives and keeping their employment.

As for the ordinary citizens in the private sector, how does such corruption affect them? I will give you a typical example. Imagine an average farmer with a simple problem from a remote village; or else a poor Fulani herdsman rearing herds of cattle coming to the city to find solutions to some problems along the lines of his profession. Mind you these two groups form the economic breadbasket of the nation. Together they form one of the two most important alternatives to Oil in retaining the country's socio-economic development base. Let us say, the person's problem calls for interaction with his elected representatives or governmental official. He comes into town in need of help and support for a problem associated with his profession for which he cannot find the means to solving them at his village.

When he has to deal with government officials, he is first neglected and kept for hours in the waiting room, if not days. When and if he finally makes it to the official in charge, he is forced to pay bribe before he gains access to a service he is entitled to by right. What is wrong with this picture? Any public office is a trust; that is a reality. The person occupying the office has been entrusted to serve the people and bring them much good, but the opposite is happening - where the official not only oppresses them but forces them to serve him, while stealing from them. What is wrong with that picture? Please forgive my being so frank and practical. Can I be real with you today? Are we ready to face the truth?

How corruption became endemic

Those grossly unjust and inhumane practices by people in elected governmental positions, appointed and also private positions, when they started years ago, were not checked. Gradually they became acceptable ways of doing business. As time went by, people's attitude towards running official positions changed. To the ordinary Nigerian today that is how a government works. Those practices, as reprehensible as they are, were seen as no big deal, to the extent that a citizen of Nigeria will pay his way from a remote area to the city for medical treatment, fall on the hospital floor and die while waiting to be served. The hospital employees have simply neglected him. People around the person will just cover his head, step over the corpse to continue their businesses as if nothing has happened. When accidents happen on Nigerian roads today, people rush towards the vehicle, on many occasions not to help victims though, but to steal their valuables from them as they lie dying.

To make matters worse, by contemporary Nigerian Psyche, the herdsman who by the way feeds hundreds of people annually through his profession and hard work, and the rural farmer who does likewise, are inferior in status by far to the city dweller. We tend to forget that every piece of meat from the daily meals of all 120 million Nigerians is raised and reared predominantly by the much underrated and undervalued herdsman. Most city dwellers however work easy unproductive jobs today. We know this because productive city jobs such as manufacturing do not happen at any significant rate in Nigeria. Therefore, most city jobs could be accomplished with strokes of a pen, rather than hard productive work.

Many contribute nothing professionally to their country's economy, but vain talk, gossip, slander and idleness; only to walk into an office and with the connivance of an official of the government, walk out with millions of Naira from people's money through concocted and non-existence contracts meant to enrich that person and the official. The twisted scenario described above makes no sense; but to date it continues to become acceptable societal norm. Only a lost people, who have lost a sense of what value is, will accept that culture, but it thrives in Nigeria.

As I work on this paper, I was captivated by headlines that continue to capture our attention every single day, involving exorbitant amounts of money. One reads "EFCC Probes Health agency over 400 million Naira stationery purchase in one month!" (*Daily Trust*, July 2008). Similar headlines run daily in our papers. This however belongs to the category of robbery by governmental personnel. And then there is another category;- private contractors. One such headline reads "Contractors abscond with silos (worth) 11.4 million pounds Sterling (2.7 billion Naira), (*Daily Trust*, July 2008).[1] For any one such incident that made headlines, only God knows how many others have not yet been discovered. Has anyone sat down to calculate the enormous loss to the economy and citizens of Nigeria in general? At such rate of public robbery, embezzlement and misappropriation, even if Nigerians are individually made of money, they will easily exhaust themselves to bankruptcy.

To return to our premise, by continually neglecting that internally designed compass that guides to our devine part, and a sense of right and wrong (*Fitra*), the public servant, elected or appointed has subverted God's own justice upon which He created and arranged His universal laws. Whether we like it or not, our personal desires, corruption, distorted and misdirected willpower as Nigerians, if pitched against God's fundamental law upon which he created the Universe, they do not stand a chance. Such actions will not only lead us nowhere, but may become the beginning of the end of our prosperity and development. The Quran says:

(a) "Do they not reflect in their own minds? Not but for just ends and for a term appointed, did Allah create the heavens and the earth, and all between them: yet are there truly many among men who deny the meeting with their Lord (at the Resurrection)!" (Surah- Ar-Room, Chapter # 30, Verse # 8) **(b)** Another similar verse from the Quran says "We created not the heavens and the earth and all between them but for just ends, and for a Term Appointed: But those who reject Faith turn away from that whereof they are warned." (Surah- Al-Ahqaf, Chapter # 46, Verse # 3); and **(c)** Finally, another verse that says "We created them not except for just ends: but most of them do not understand." (Surah- Ad-Dukhan, Chapter # 44, Verse # 39).[2]

Many verses clearly state that the backbone or blueprint for the creation of the whole universe, not just our earth is living together while maintaining and according justice to every one and every being. So anyone who thinks he can continue to ride against the tide, contrary to

---

[1] Daily Trust (online edition), monitored July 20, 2008.
[2] Abdullahi Yusuf Ali translation of the Holy Qur'an

universal laws in existence long before we found ourselves here, is doomed to failure; and mass failure if I may add. Where justice is denied, peace will find no place. And where peace is non-existence, and insecurity is the norm, there will simply be no prosperity.

The Problems

The main and urgent problems could be sub-divided into two major parts. The first is the disease (illness) or what you may rightfully call negative underlying causes. The second group comprises of the problems that manifested themselves (symptoms) as a result of those underlying causes.

Causes
1. Corruption.
2. Loss of values and a sense of who we are (social & ethical Problem).
3. Moral and ethical decay powered by greed (self-Centeredness).
4. No patriotism, powered by utter disregard for the values that binds us as a community i.e. (Love of nation and its people).
5. Lack of commitment and non-challant attitude towards important issues of state.

Result

6. No sustainability (developmental continuity).
7. No accountability (holding people accountable for actions and funds).
8. No adequate research, effective planning, and implementation.
9. Applying simple solutions to complex problems.

Causes

We have pretty much covered systemic corruption, though I wish we have more time on that because that is the major underlying cancer gnawing slowly at the fabric of Nigeria's development and prosperity. Generally, management worldwide connotes two basic ideas. Trying to make productive, a conflicting situation, i. e. diverse employees with differing ideas on the one hand, and lack of resources to adequately implement those ideas on the other. In fact management as a term implies dealing with inadequate resources.[3] As far as the disagreements, it consists of; conflict of interests between various units of a ministry or company (research and development unit, personnel, line producers etc); differing ideas, inadequate resources etc. A good manager globally is he who best "manages" these typical challenges most effectively.

In Nigeria however, these challenges are further complicated by a crippling mind-set. (a) That resources allocated to an office or its branch are meant to go to the managers pockets, with the crumbs going into the mid- and lower level employees pockets. (b) That government resources are open to waste and embezzlement by those entrusted with it. Government work process is so choked with bribery and kick backs so much so that even to get its statutory allocated funds, a ministry or unit of a larger organization is forced to engage in kickbacks at every level of the process.[4] The Minister plays along because the mindset is once the money got released; they first deduct what they paid in bribery, and what is left of it personally belongs to them, with no dividend going towards working for the country and its people.

These kinds of activities cripple genuine development and productivity. It seeps deep down eating away at the motivation of competent employees willing to come up with ideas to deal with genuine challenges the country faces, be it electricity generation, adequate water supply or simply producing or encouraging the production of enough food by our farmers. Nigerians are smart, but they cannot put their intellect to use in such a setting. As daunting as these problems are, anyone who comes out with the solutions is looked upon as the person who betrayed his colleagues by divulging their secret system of personally enriching and milking both the system and the ordinary

---

[3] For details of areas that managers deal with generally, see Montana, P. J. & Charnov, B H., (2000) Management. New York: Barron's Educational Series, Inc.

[4] "Members of the public had to bribe their way through in the ministries and parastatals to get attention and one government agency had to bribe another government agency to obtain release of its statutory allocation of funds. The impact of official corruption is so rampant....it has distorted and retrogressed development." President Obasanjo's inaugural speech, May 1999.

citizen. Nigerians otherwise compete in Schools and colleges worldwide coming home with trophies in terms of ability to analyze and come up with solutions to problems in all professional areas.

Unfortunately as smart and intelligent as Nigerians are in their string of degrees from various national and international universities, they seem at a loss when they visit their colleagues for seminars and conferences in comparable offices abroad. The reason is not problem solving skills or disparity in intellectual capability, but that the delusional and intentional crippling of their own system at home made them appear daft and unresourceful as they tour foreign facilities. And even after spending resources for them to learn how other countries confront similar problems, they generally lack the willpower and courage to initiate a change at their home offices afterwards. So ultimately, Nigerian managers find themselves obtaining a failing grade in the field of effective management not because they are daft and unresourceful intellectually, but by personal greed and systemic complications prevalent in their home communities.

The next issue is the loss of values, dignity and a sense of worth. This is an important point. Long gone are the days when people are proud of who they are and the values they hold. The general mass of the people today, approximately 70-80 percent of the population who do not belong to the elite i.e. the educated managers in appointed positions or elected ones have been made either deliberately by design or by the contemporary value system prevalent in Nigeria today, to think that they cannot (a) think for themselves; (b) effectively figure out what is going on or going wrong with their government; (c) that power, positions, government decisions, and government processes are so complicated for them to understand or do something about. The result is a passive citizenry and working class with no self-esteem or motivation to rise up to the challenge and proactively work towards ensuring justice, peace and prosperity for themselves, and their children.

The mindset described above has to be urgently reversed. It does no one any good at all. Before the breakdown of our value system, there was much peace, order, tranquility and security. You cannot even begin to compare those days 60s – 70s to what has become of the country. The older value system stresses respect for elders in the community and home, parents, grandparents etc. The family is knit together, the community and ultimately the country at large bond with each other. These people may not have acquired formal education, but they are smart, wise and gifted with a lot of wisdom (*Hikma*). They can sit anyone down and relate to them the seeping problems unfolding as they observe them, and also the best way to go about solving them. They can analyze possible pitfalls with each and every decision they give you. Instead of working together with them, today's generation feel they are inferior, old fashioned, and cannot think wisely because they have no formal education. The result is a "disconnect" between generations that has hurt the country bad.

Their counsel as to what is morally and ethically right is neglected, so much so that more and more people today continue to move away from long held values sanctioned by universal laws of righteousness and good conduct that breeds community building and progress. In fact the people with long and proud history of community building and orderly living align themselves today with communities that do not have such background in order to learn from them the art of scamming, cheating and acquiring ill gotten wealth overnight regardless of how one does it. Please excuse my being real today with the facts unfolding in Nigeria. If we want change we have to identify the root causes and deal with them.

The decaying value system runs smack into the next underlying cause, i.e. lack of patriotism. By that we undervalue the important values that bind us as a community. In fact the last few years after fighting hard to restore democracy and the rule of the majority, different sectors of the country try to hammer divisive issues, mostly based on greed. They do that in political, economic and social arenas. The call for sovereign conference at a time when elected officials took office for the first time after many years of struggle to restore democracy is one example. How one could neglect an elected government and prefer that delegates be nominated to discuss any agenda that determines such very important issues of the nation is an enigma only those who spearheaded the call know.

Lack of patriotism is also fanned by many of the articulated problems. When people despair of their leaders and their motives, sometimes patriotism is the culprit. It is hard for individuals to maintain patriotism for any reasonable period when they are embarrassed almost always by news of what either their elected leaders or those in position of representing the image of Nigeria to the world are engaged in. When the name of the country is dragged in the mud, it affects how people feel. It does hurt them, but gradually as human behavior shows, people tend to distance themselves to any persistent cause of grief. Improving and taking actions to jumpstart and sustain the solution to Nigerian socio-economic problems, should help boost its acceptance in patriotic terms by the general public.

Finally in the list of causes is a lack of commitment and non-challant attitude towards important issues of state. Generally, issues of governance, even if they directly affect the welfare of the people, are not given adequate attention. A typical example is the issue of sustainable power. As important as the issue is, and as much as the government and people in position to do something about it are trying to convince us that it is insurmountable, we do know that is a fairly tale. Countries much poorer than Nigeria, with no financial resources have done it. Furthermore apart from the funds to do it, Nigeria has all the tangible resources for generating electricity e.g. large rivers, coal, gas and oil resources. How can they credibly convince us that they cannot provide sustainable and uninterrupted power supply for their people? Bear with me, in a short while as we go along I intend to point at where some of such solutions lie.

Results

Mischievous misuse of sustainability as an excuse in 1999 – at the inception of the current round of civilian administration - has caused the country much distress. While sustainability of the newly regained democratic system of governance is important to meaningful development, it should not deter progress. We also require sustainability and steady progress in socio-economic terms. The Nigerian government however, especially the immediate past administration, has misused the sustainability of the so called "nascent" democracy to hoodwink the country into virtual pacification. People deserve to see responsible progress for the 11 years of democratic governance in Nigeria.

One of the realities of governance (as enumerated and supported by Quranic verses we quoted earlier), is that continuity can only be guaranteed if rooted strongly in justice and transparence. What would you expect of a new manager coming in to find an office full of redundant, unworkable and probably ill conceived projects that were brought to life not because of genuine demand for them, but in order to enrich the former manager and his clique among the contractors in the private sector? There is absolutely no reason for the new Manager to work towards building on the former manager's foundation. Why? A host of reasons, among them: a) those inherited baggage only add to the present manager's impediments. The continuance of the old projects or tasks becomes a waste of resources with no results. (b) The new manager is not solving the real problems and tasks assigned to the office; so in the end people will accuse him of inefficiency (c) He is not contributing to his own legacy and portfolio for which others may later judge him in that same position, or recommend him for future positions. (d) He is not working towards pleasing those who gave him the position. Remember that the choice of any leader or employer reflects the on the judgment of the person who employed him to the position. And betrayal of that trust and service also reflects on the employer and all those who put in a word of reference for the new manager in order to get the position.

One main problem that always baffles me is, we tend to believe that a new government will be different only to find our hopes dashed. It has never surprised me and should not surprise anyone. The general attitude of the overwhelming population is reflected in leaders and appointees, and verse-versa. No one should expect to reap tomatoes from a field he has planted potatoes; like begets like. We need to admit and face squarely that the generality of Nigerians including those in public service are becoming increasingly ethically bankrupt. The ethical and moral reasons are clear.[5] Our elected and appointed leaders will always come from the same ethically bankrupt society. It is delusional therefore, to

---

[5] Matharat-al-Qulub by Imam al Maulud translated by Hamza Yusuf in the book titled "Purification of the Heart," Starlight Press (2004) ""Covetousness, the desire to aggress and exploit, the longing to pilfer natural resources, the inordinate love of wealth and position and other maladies are a manifestation of diseases found nowhere but in the heart. Every criminal, miser, abuser, scoffer, embezzler and hateful person does what he or she does because of a diseased heart....so if we want to change our world, we do not begin by rectifying the outward."

expect miracles from them. The only way is to work on restoring ethical conduct and eradicating all these counterproductive practices nationwide.

How do we eradicate the problems? You may ask. We start by defining, enumerating and publicizing on top of our voices the issues that are crippling the nation's prosperity and make it an important topic of open discussion. We then embark on a mass campaign for attitudinal changes backed by the enforcement of all our anti-corruption laws at the same time. Negative forces and bad conduct love to grow in darkness and secrecy. Clearly articulate the problems without fear or favor. I assure you, any government that does that, while credibly suggesting and applying remedies will win the goodwill of the people. Only then will its importance be marched equally by resources aimed at eradicating it. We may then be able to implement carefully thought out and measurable plan for a mass campaign to publicize the evils in open as well as subliminal ways.

The electronic media, mostly government owned could be put into greater use, through for example, highly captivating drama series exposing such unethical practices how one can recognize them along with their consequences for the society. Public announcements using proverbial and carefully chosen metaphorical jargons deep rooted in the culture of the local audience may be used during the campaign for effectiveness. Regularly produced and widely televised documentaries that focus on targeted issues relating to awareness as well as uprooting such degenerative practices should also be a priority.

Another problem that surfaced from the causes enumerated above is lack of accountability. Nigeria has become a nation of investigative committees, committee of inquiries and ongoing investigations. Hardly do you see prosecutions following those investigations, and rarely do people get charged. The public knows a crime has been committed, they know their allocated funds have disappeared without any tangible gain from it. The government officials elected or appointed to manage it know it is missing, but ultimately the public is pacified by committees of enquiries that ultimately turn up nothing.

Even in cases where such committees of inquiries do turn up something, nothing is done by way of recovering the funds and bringing it back to the people from whom it was misappropriated. In short such committees are usually temporary popularity schemes for those who set them up, only to become a blackmailing team who end up sharing the loot with the original embezzlers. The poor citizens never get their money back to fix their schools and fund their hospitals. As a result, their welfare institutions continue to deteriorate. Where then is the accountability, fairness and justice?

There is absolutely no way you can maintain peace and security without justice, even in a simpler group such as a family, let alone complex communities. Such actions breed insecurity. Very soon some of the frustrated citizens will not obey laws. Those with little discipline and moral upbringing begin to set up road blocks, to gain something for themselves by force. In such unruly situations the innocent citizens fall victim again to such actions.

When important issues such as portable water and electricity are brought to light, they just draw headlines from those empowered to resolve it. They give speeches to the public as to how they promise to resolve it soon. But ordinary Nigerians have now become so discouraged that anyone can ever do something about such debilitating problems they face every single day. One of the major issues in that regard is inadequate research, planning and brainstorming until a viable and applicable solution is found. Because people want to take credit unnecessarily, they are impatient to seek workable even if long term solutions.

Nigerians as enumerated earlier can match every single country in terms of intellectual capability of its people. But that resource is not used. A team of academicians professionally knowledgeable in the area could be asked for example to join a team that may include, professional electrical engineers with hands on experience in public service, energy experts in areas of hydro electric generation, coal energy acquisition and use experts, energy distribution experts etc down to those with a host of experience in hands-on issues of resolving interruptions etc.

Today in management, teambuilding is key to resolving the most intricate problems.[6] That team does not look down or undervalue any employee. If solutions being sought affects any unit, everyone including the lowest level worker in that unit finds a place at the table to air his or her views, and such views are seriously considered. Once the team is made up, it is then given a time limit, task, resources that should be available, and told to come up with a blueprint that resolves all the problems that have already been identified and enumerated. In reality however, politics once again coupled with greed becomes the motivating factor. In the end nothing gets done because the right way of tackling the issue is deliberately circumvented for personal greed.

Solutions

Because of time, we will just run through some possible solutions without necessarily explaining them in detail.

1. Mass campaign could be launched to deprogram the general public away from deep rooted psyche and actions that are counterproductive. These should include public announcements, captivating drama series, and documentaries by the nation's broadcast media.
2. Careful scrutiny in the choice of People who lead or serve at critical and important positions. Leadership and servitude should be given to people who not only possess knowledge, but those who have demonstrated trustworthiness and piety (*Taqwa*). Pious enough to know their responsibilities, i.e. the burden from the people and their Devine Lord to whom they will be accountable to someday.

3. Transparency and openness in governmental transactions is essential. An informed public is generally active and participative.[7] Gone are the days when papers print annual allocations to every state government; including the Federal budget as allocated to federal ministries. Followed by state government's allocations to various

---

[6] David, K.C., Kelvin, J.H., & William, J.T., (1996) Managing the Change Process. New York: McGraw-Hill, Pg. 19.
[7] Advantages of openness and participation include, enhanced motivation, better decision results, creates trust, accelerated progress towards goal achievement. Motivation & Goal-Setting (1993) second edition New Jersey: Career Press, Inc. Pg.63

ministries and the local governments. That allows the public to set adequate demands from their public office holders in terms of project priorities: and also demand accountability.

4. Strict enforcement of accountability at federal and state government levels.

5. For patriotism: Establishment of various projects with the intention of instilling some degree of love of community and country. Games and Sports is one such means that brings a city, state or country together for the common purpose of winning. Mutual projects between neighboring states to harness common resources for their people's development. Interstate visits and coalitions for associations of common interest across state lines. Interregional alliances and student exchange. National Youth Service has helped a lot in that regard.

Conclusion

In summary, the socio-economic problems are pervasive and require a mass campaign to redirect our energies. Eradicating corruption and attitude change are the key. And before anything we need to start working on ourselves personally. Charity begins at home is an adage commonly spoken of in Nigeria. Though one's means of livelihood with which he eats and feeds his children as most will probably agree should be clean, most do not view the evil practices that corrupts their subsistence source as they should "evil." People make excuses such as, well everyone takes bribe. Everyone has to be paid money under the table in order to perform the same job they are paid by the government to do anyway. Others will not see any evil in concocting a fake event or contract, allocating money to it, then paying themselves subsequently. Well everyone does it, they will tell you.

The realities and the evil generated by such activities are immense. They are the root of all underdevelopment, disease, death, malnutrition, lack of education and degeneration of same etc. A nation blessed has cursed itself by its hand and actions. For every penny you take out of the money entrusted to you through the office you occupy, and the ones you take from ordinary people who had to double pay you (salary and bribe) in order to perform your duty, you will be asked to account for it one day. In one way or another you will, if not beginning in this world, you will at the hands of Him that created you. This is not the position of just one religion, but even the atheist believes in what they call the Karma effect; that is to say what you send into the world of your deeds good or bad, will come back to you. Examples of that phenomenon abound around us. Yet people take these issues lightly generally, and it should not be the case at all. An attitude change in that direction will go a long way in redirecting our energies to nation building.

Breathing Life into the Economy: Lessons from Japan and China

Hadiza Wada, DBA

September 5, 2009

Nigerians aught to understand that nations of the world that drastically changed their economies for the better, and within the shortest time possible, did not get there by taking cosmetic measures. We have already discussed that Nigeria is not making headway because its people simplify complex issues and build on such shaky foundation, only to react when they fail. There is the need to be proactive not reactive. That is what helped nations that used to be considered among the third world just years ago, changed their destiny within a decade or even less.

Such exemplary nations took strong turnaround measures to combat what they rightfully understood to be huge deep rooted problems. They rightfully understood that they were heading somewhere they do not want to go. And that dancing to the tune of every other drummer (nations) to the detriment of their peoples' immediate and long term needs and interest is not right and cannot be just. So instead of treating the symptoms of a disease, and neglecting the disease itself, they correctly diagnose the problems that led them to developing that disease, weigh their potentials as a nation, then changed everything including attitude, negative environmental influence, going after what they lack in resources to stay healthy even if from other countries, etc.

Take the example of Japan, a nation that arguably, first taught the world in the twentieth century that you do not even have to be endowed with natural resources to become a rich and prosperous nation. Japan literally imports every major resource it needs to keep its industries running. Its geo-physical characteristics are harsh, and unyielding. Its land capacity is also limited. But it realized it has a large population to take care of, and it also has the knowledge, and capability technologically to compete with any other nation. So it invested in its knowledge and population, then embarked on the art of getting what it needed from others to feed its industries, until it became a worldwide force industrially in some aspects, and beat every other nation in manufacturing the most durable, fuel efficient, and economically viable cars in the whole world. And that was a nation devastated by World War II, and made a pariah state earlier that same century.

China most recently has surprised the world, including the industrialized nations. It has today taken a seat among the most powerful nations on the planet. Not long ago, China was well behind. It was being bombarded by criticisms of human rights abuses, closing its doors to modernism and capitalism. You do not even sit on the same table and dine with China, without drawing criticisms from the Western Countries. It was also criticized for its monetary as well as economic policies. I was in its capital Beijing in 1995, and the city though modern by some standards, does appear to be struggling with a population beyond its capacity. That was readily apparent from the faces of the people on the street, the polluted air, and the conditions of the high rise apartments, with clothes hanging on balconies and broken windows. A decade later when I returned to the city, Beijing has more than doubled its modernity and affluence. You just cannot compare the two eras. In fact I would confidently say, Beijing today looks more attractive than many major cities United States is proud of.

The most important lesson to learn from both is that you do not succeed as quickly as those two nations did, without taking the unconventional way. Window dressing and patch-patch solutions employed to maintain the status quo, while expecting different results does not work. Playing the same game expecting different results – at the same time looking for approval from nations competing with you openly in the market, is never a wise idea. These two nations realized that. And they were not the only ones out there who dramatically changed for the better. We just mentioned them as an example.

The two nations chose a strategy of charting original workable solutions to address their unique and original problems. Then they succeeded. They were criticized, sometimes harshly, and sometimes even maneuvers were employed to see them fail, but they dug in hard, and were willing to sweat it through. As Einstein described to the world, the difference between a genius and one who is not is persistence. When you know what you want and set out to achieve it, failures are only opportunities for learning how not to go about it the next time. And criticisms from your competitors are sometimes reassurances that you are making headway. You just persist and persevere.

One of the most important areas China appeared to have developed is almost similar to that of Japan. It began an aggressive program of putting its vast population to work. It also set out to aggressively acquire the resources it does not have, to feed those industries. China, a communist country, did it the best way they knew how. The government cleared the land, set up industries all over the country, then leases or rents them to its people to produce whatever it is they have the market for. A government spoon fed industrialization if you might call it that, a unique way that probably is a pioneering one, never implemented before. Whether filling some international orders for individual companies or people, where the money was readily available to them, or else loaning the funds to manufacture products and sell them to other countries where markets for them exists; the Chinese people have a chance to utilize such amenities. They helped revolutionized their country within a short span of time.

The result was, before long, China was producing so much goods in every category and choking markets across the world. It was moreover able to sell so cheap that people were willing to forsake other goods for Chinese imports. China did not apply bandage to a wound it knows has been growing, gearing towards malignancy. It studied the problem which allowed the wound to develop in the first place, and then went after it with zeal. Everything now within just about a decade, appears to be in their favor. China today has the highest trade surplus with the United States, the world's largest economy; including financial sector credit (i.e. makes it the top country U.S. owes in dollar amount). It has long unseated Japan in that regard.

What is glaringly clear from events and actions that continue to grace the pages of Nigeria's newspapers and media every single day is that, those who control resources, policy, and application of both, tend to neglect or conveniently ignore the seriousness of the condition the country is in. This neglect covers all aspects of existence, be it social, economic, political, cultural and commerce. Those in a position to steer the nation, tend to want to maintain the status quo, as if the status of Nigeria today is okay. They play "survival" reacting and consequently just bending to every wind that blows around them, without any regard to serious analysis and application of important industrial and commercial policies. When they ran into problems that crop from their neglect of impending issues, they rush to "fix" it, only for it to emerge again.

I believe that any nation is able, with the right leadership and the right attitude among its citizens, to grow its economy for the better. In the case of Nigeria, I do not believe the nation has a problem of self-esteem, where the policy makers think Nigeria cannot think for itself and chart its course commensurate with its peculiarities. Nigerians are some of the most pragmatic, bold and practical people on individual level. Take them anywhere in the world, they will learn how to survive in a heart beat. They may not apply that gifted wisdom and intellect the right way all the time, but they will teach everyone a thing or two, including those living on that land for generations. That gift of wits and intellect may not be unconnected to the art of surviving their domestic ordeal for years.

It is the policy makers, and their patrons within the elite, who continue to ignore the issues. They have within their power and influence the command for human as well as financial resources to plan and implement such laudable ventures, but have failed the nation. They have long disconnected themselves from the citizens they were supposed to serve, or the problems those citizens want addressed. Probably, they feel they are comfortable with the status quo, even as they watch all institutions fail one after the other.

Those in leadership and the rich have an outlet, because they can send their children abroad for school, or send family members and themselves abroad for medical care, as educational as well as health care facilities continue to fail. They do not receive their electorate in their offices, neither do they set up offices that receive and process genuine complaints from the public. And they do not have the initiative to analyze problems by themselves, even though that is not the best democratic route, and decide what problems are endemic under their jurisdiction so they can eliminate them in the interest of the people.

The leadership, including most of the elite, are at par with most of their counterparts among the well read and intelligent academia in the nation's universities generally, and some within the general public who know the facts of history and are well versed with current affairs. While the academia and well informed public find such inactions repulsive, the leadership and elite are drunk with the art of mimicking and trying to please foreign countries in all their actions. They yearn for the endorsement and approval of foreign powers, not the people they serve and are responsible for. This they do furthermore, regardless of policies of such foreign governments towards Nigeria or the continent as a whole. The question is, how far can you improve while trying to impress a foreign interest; or in short someone you are not and can never be? If you have an ailment called A, and you witness someone with an ailment called B mixing and taking the medicine that was made to cure his ailment called B, because it is an important question of survival, I do not expect you to foolishly buy that same medicine to take while you know you have a different ailment from his.

The problem of misdiagnosis or non interest in credible and serious diagnosis has permeated succeeding administrations in Nigeria and continues to date. And without original diagnosis, and application of original solutions, Nigeria continues to just dance to the tune of every drummer that comes onto its shores. Nigeria is celebrating half a century of self government this year, 2010. But to date, the government for the most part just reacts to the winds that blow its way, with no motivation of its own, to build the nation.

Solutions

The first fix in reviving and ensuring a vibrant economy is strong and sustainable industrial policy and a plan to implement it effectively. The industrial policy of Nigeria needs drastic fixing. Just as we mentioned before, there are no serious steps by the authorities to address issues of industrialization. No serious studies have been conducted into that sector, as important as it is to general prosperity. In cases where there are, with the result that those industries have survived, there seems to be no coordination between the policy and its practicality to allow them to prosper. The export import policy either scuttles the industries, or else counterproductive policies that strangle the industries are employed and implemented rigorously.

What do other serious nations do? They prioritize based on where their foreign exchange earnings usually gets depleted, one after the other, and go to work on it. If for example the nation is bleeding hard currency into textile to cloth its teeming population, and its agricultural researchers say the nation has enough arable land to produce the cotton needed to run weaving and clothes making industries within the nation, that policy becomes enacted immediately, implemented and defended with all the laws of the land. It is that serious.

It is a serious crime for any government policy to neglect its people, enriching other nations while its population is so frustrated by unemployment. The government must become the watchdog for public interest at all costs, not personal and self enriching interests. Even, when bad season comes or the farmers overproduce the commodity so much so that the industries could not consume all, thereby lowering the market price and profit for the farmer, the federal government buys off the cotton at a profit for the farmer, then sells it to the industries at regular prices, and exports the surplus abroad even if at a loss. That ensures continuous production of raw material for the country's industries. It gives the farmer confidence that there will always be a buyer for his produce, and it also assures a living for the industrial textile worker who will continue to enjoy uninterrupted employment. The United States to date subsidizes cotton farmers as well as other food crops to help self-sufficiency in feeding its population annually and Europe does the same to its cattle farmers. And these are rich industrialized nations.

Industrialization is the key. Growing your own food for consumption, and setting up industries to produce and satisfy at least some of the most crucial demands from your population for clothing, shelter, and other basic necessities is the way forward for any nation serious about development.

Nigerian Industrial Challenges

Hadiza Wada, DBA ...April 3, 2010

Nigerian Industries have been undergoing a steady but rapid decline. According to most sources used in this paper, one of the most severe blows that crippled Nigerian Industries was the introduction of a program from IMF and the World Bank titled the Structural Adjustment Program SAP. The program plus subsequent policies of the federal government, especially those related to export and import policies, and the provision and maintenance of adequate infrastructure were others.

Relative to other Sub Saharan countries, Nigeria is pretty much well ahead industrially. Most developing nations up to about nineteen seventies were attracting only those industries that manufacture what one may call, the non-essentials. It was quite clear that the developed nations were not interested in allowing them industrialized realistically. They sabotage all efforts for realistic industrialization so they can guarantee (a) a market for their own goods, and (b) keep nations weak and subservient so they could use them as stooges on international issues. When you look at the ratio of industries many such countries have, they tend to be in non essential products such as beverages (usually coca-cola, and other locally named soda). Nigeria even at that time had a few more types of industries manufacturing some of the essentials every nation needs, including pharmaceuticals, textile, shoes and leatherworks, plastics and others. When it comes to Nigeria, the drawback usually is inability to produce a significant percentage of such goods to satisfy even reasonable demands for them.

Today however, Nigeria could do much better than its present position. It appears that more private businesses and investment companies are interested in setting up even more industries, but they appear to face some real challenges that make it difficult to actualize their dream. Bashir Borodo, President of the Manufacturing Association of Nigeria MAN described the challenges manufacturers face in Nigeria. It includes lack of adequate funding; diminishing power supply forcing manufacturers to rely on individual power generating alternatives run on price hiked gas (inadequate). According to Borodo:

> "Transportation costs due to bad roads, police check points and the spiraling costs of fuel have helped to cripple manufacturing. Bad roads, unfriendly industrial policies by government and non-availability of raw materials, have all combined to drive 355 industries out of 385 MAN members from Imo and Abia states in less than 11 years of Nigeria's democratic government."

Kano, the home base of Bashir is the second largest manufacturing city in Nigeria, after its port city of Lagos. A paper co-written by two members of Bayero University Staff from Kano, Dr. Badayi Sani and Sa'id Suleiman Senior and Principal Lecturers of Economics respectively, also described many factors that have contributed to crippling the manufacturing base of Kano and the country in general. *"Though, the state has witnessed a massive decline in its industries, and industrial activities, in line with the national trend, the state can still boast of over 350 large and medium industries."* Such industries include Food processing, Clothing and Textile; Pharmaceuticals, Paper Mills and Stationery, Plastic, Metalwork and Tannery.

Among the crippling policies highlighted by the paper are (a) wrong and inconsistent monetary policies of the federal Government. One of such policies was also an IMF imposed one, i.e. devaluation of the national currency. It came with the Structural Adjustment Program package of the IMF in the 1980s. Its liberalization policy made cost of money or loan expensive (because regulatory issues were relaxed and left to the banks) and made it possible for banks to engage in business with less patriotic businesses that move capital away from industries and farming. Such liberalization policy of IMF was described by the duo in the following words:

> "This policy in the name of making our industries competitive internationally has also caused industrial decline not only in Kano but in the whole country. Given the state of

our industries and the environment in which they operate, there is no way we can make them compete on equal terms with more mature and long established industries with superior and higher quality products from South East Asia and other advanced countries." (Drs Sani, Sulaiman, BUK)

The second reason relates to infrastructural decay. This includes inadequacy of power supply, network of roads, and the deterioration and failure to rehabilitate the rail system. "The lack of telecommunication services particularly in Chalawa and part of Sharada and Tokarawa / Jogana areas" has also been cited as one of the factors responsible for the collapse of industries in Kano. "The role of telecommunication in speeding up the process of ordering and delivery of goods both finished and un-finished products or raw materials can not be overemphasized."

A trend is reported to have begun in Kano, where businesses especially those belonging to immigrants from foreign countries have started relocating. BBC reported recently that factories such as Holborn Textiles and Lakonda Furniture have moved to neighboring countries such as Ghana where the infrastructural capacity is not so affected. A local official of MAN in Kano, Ali Madugu, told BBC that about 60% of the problems manufacturers in the city face could be traced back to lack of electricity. Another source says even the industries still in business today in Kano, which he put the figure at about 150, do so at a fraction of their usual capacities, citing that most have to depend on government patronage to survive.

In Kaduna, the major problem is the closure of the textile industries. After about 43 years of ongoing fight to remain open, in October 2007 the United Nigeria Textile Ltd (UNTL) finally closed it doors and had to let go thousands of its employees. As per an article about it run by the *Daily Trust* and written by Sani Babadoko at that time, at the time of UNTL's closing, it was operating at about thirty percent of its capacity. The Kaduna headquartered textile industry established two years after independence from foreign rule started in 1962 with Kaduna Textiles limited, which soon became the igniter for rapid expansion to many others such as Arewa Textiles, UNTL, Finetex, Nortex, Unitex and Supertex in Kaduna.

The provision of food, clothing and shelter is paramount to any nation and its governmental activity. The reason covers all aspects from social to economic. Kaduna textile was partially fulfilling that basic need for clothing. Today however, due mainly to bad industrial policies, cheaper imported textiles have flooded the market, forcing closures and teeming unemployment for the industry. The Asian countries were backed by their comparative advantages such as good infrastructures, better export incentives at home and cheap labor in their countries. According to Babadoko:

> "Trouble started for the industry with the introduction of the Structural Adjustment Program (SAP) in the 1980s. The program imposed by the Bretton Woods institutions (World Bank and the International Monetary Fund, IMF) prescribed the removal of all barriers to trade, removal of all subsidies on goods and services. Soon the cost of production escalated. The deregulation regime also excluded protection for the local industries, including textiles. The Asian textile companies, especially those from China quickly took advantage of this and started flooding Nigerian markets with sub-standard fabrics. Recent reports indicate that China exports over 40 million meters of fabric into Africa with over 70 per cent coming to Nigeria." (*Daily Trust*)

According to a UNTL manager some of the real problems with even the 30% capacity they struggled to produce include, "brazen activities of smugglers of textile products and infringement of our trademarks and designs on smuggled goods have worsened the situation "… **our traditional markets have been flooded with smuggled cheaper but inferior fabrics, often passed on as our products."**

With problems such as these no industry will find the motivation, in spite of the lure of profit and continuing job provision for people, to continue to survive. Governmental policy is the problem, period. Nations ordinarily push their population towards industrialization with the main purpose of internally satisfying the nation's needs. Even when problems such as these emerge suddenly, they require strong governmental backing.

No serious government in the world will sign the dotted line on any program they frankly know will strangle their industries, nor sit idle while such problems become endemic. It should get into emergency gear as soon as it realizes the problems with immediate enactment and implementation of policies and legislations. The cooperation of the nation's citizens in curbing smuggling is another area that needs to be stressed.

Lagos State at the Southern Gulf Port of Nigeria is the most industrialized city of the country. One major reason it continued to sustain its lead is its location as a major port city on the West African coast. For longer periods it was catering for not just Nigeria but neighboring countries' needs. It provides to this day the ease of importation and exportation. But Lagos has also suffered most of the same ailments.

Writing in September 2009, Modupe Ogunbayo enumerated some of the problems generally faced by Lagos industries. Giving an example of a polyester textile plant inside the Spintex Company Limited, located in Lagos she disclosed how they moved from full manufacturing within the country providing employment, training and know how to Nigerians, to importation of the same textiles made by other rival industries abroad due to governmental monetary policies (IMF and World Bank imposed).

Banking and the prevailing import-export policies have virtually strangled such industries, thereby allowing the influx of imports by their former competition in Asia. Even multinational companies such as PZ have had its share of such problems. According to Ogunbayo's sources PZ's recent mass layoff of staff will soon be followed by an overhaul where they will reorganize and come out as importers of the same goods they use to manufacture within the country. They also chose that line because that is the only way they could turn a profit in their line of work. 40 companies in the area of non metallic products such as pharmaceuticals, tire, shoes etc have also closed their operations within just one year, laying off over 80,000 employees. These include Dunlop, Michelin, Mercury, Pfizer, etc.

One of the most affected that should really be lamented, even by the accounts from the Lagos article, is the textile industries which were mostly located in the northern states of the country. The reason given by Paul Olarewaju, the Director General of the Nigerian Textile Manufacturers Association NTMA is because it is one of the industries that has become truly Nigerianized industrially speaking. It generally utilizes locally produced raw materials such as cotton from local farmers, and chemicals (principally dye) from Nigerian chemical industries.

"Before 1997, the Nigerian textile industry was the second largest in Africa after Egypt with over 250 vibrant factories and running above 50 percent utilization capacity" says Olarewaju. But today its market share in the nation is just 20%. In a seminar convened in Kaduna to find real solutions to the textile industry, the figures revealed by the Nigerian Textile Manufacturing Association NTMA were staggering. The Nigerian Textile Manufacturers Association (NTMA) argued that "the industry, which used to be the second largest employer of labor after government has lost 577,000 workforce between 1992 and 2006."

The Role of Industrialized Countries

Though there are many things the federal government of Nigeria could do to ensure the viability and growth of Nigerian industries, we will now look deeper into the calculated role played by other industrialized countries to effectively keep it back from progress. These nations using the IMF and World Bank work behind their corporations to force developing countries onto routes that only serve the corporations' ultimate interest, to the detriment of the individual interests of single countries and their population in the developing world.

A growing number of political and economic analysts in the United States are coming to a general understanding that the nation, being the leading member of the industrialized world is targeting vulnerable countries in order to establish an empire, very much like what Great Britain was in it's glorious past. Countless books have been written about that. The writers believe U S foreign and economic policy since the times of Ronald Reagan have already started to implement such policy. Many have put those thoughts into books, so numerous to count, including NGOs, Associations etc. Analysts such as Ivan Leland, for example, wrote in 2004 "The Empire has no Clothes." Others are "A Game as Old as Empire" (Hiatt, 2007); The Secret History of the American Empire, (Perkins, 2007), and a host of others. Some within the ranks went through their own crusades, alone, to expose such ideas they oppose. One of them was Scott Ritter an Iraqi weapons inspector who later literally parted ways with his superiors.

Another group of analysts concentrate on an idea that the present global economic order is unjust and unsustainable. They hypothesize that if U S citizens continue to remain uninvolved in their governmental policy direction they would wake up one day in a world where their children will be vulnerable. Both categories of writers however divergent in their approach could be brought together under one general theme; the quest for control and economic domination of the world. One of such writers we have tabled in this publication earlier. He was an economist who was used by corporations to ensnare third world leaders into deals that will break their countries economically. The goal is to enslave foreign nations from thousands of mile away, a different tactic from the British imperial days, where they physically invaded the nations. The goals being the same however, they work towards exploiting and taking away the nation's resources. The means of doing that include convincing the nation's leaders to invest a lot of money in projects that do not benefit the nation but the foreign nations, while at the same time breaking the economy with enormous repayment terms, a double gain for them.

Their tactics of establishing white elephant projects in such countries, and engaging in big projects such as building dams and other infrastructure falls in line with today's electricity challenges Nigeria face. Nigeria has invested too much into trying to produce enough electricity to power its economy, beginning with the first government after independence that built a large dam across the third longest river on the continent (River Niger), up to the government of Olusegun Obasanjo that spent billions of dollars with which we learnt he contracted U S firms such as General Electric, but has not been able to make any significant impact in that regard. But the Obasanjo Administration has barely made a dent, as the dam built in the sixties still had the same few turbines working *(As the picture on page 57 shows only one turbine is working at the time of the picture)*. No improvement has been made.

The dumb idea that what we needed was new turbines was debugged recently when this writer learnt that much older dams than Kianji in the

US still use their turbines. What is needed to improve Kianji, is dredging the river to allow it hold much water needed to turn the existing turbines. Silt build-up is the main problem with it, followed by expanding the distribution capacity.

As for World Bank and the IMF, the game has been made much sharper, actually. The industrialized nations are not going to give up on the idea of keeping others down while they continue to pile financial and economic gains. It is proving more probable that it would have to take the victim himself, to turn the tide around. Writes Perkins late last year 2009, "Although the IMF had fallen into disrepute in the early and mid-2002, the G-20 countries had infused it with more than triple its previous capital and awarded it new mandates for power in 2008 and 2009."

Energy is the Most Crucial Issue

Now that the challenges have been outlined, we would suggest taking proactive steps irrespective of such challenges. We do know by now that reliable energy is the key to industrialization, period. It is the top issue, followed by others such as good and reliable water supply, good network of roads, warehouses, efficient ports and smooth-running transportation system. None of the above is in the state it should be in, but the most important of them, reliable power is in a crisis situation right now as we speak, and has been so for many years.

It has always been my deep belief that the energy problem in Nigeria is a result of negligence from government, and attitudinal problem (counterproductive practices that have become a habit), and not substance. The people have a part in this, in so far as the social issues such as vandalism of cables and other hardware, illegal connections which overstrains transformers causing constant breakdowns, failures and sometimes outburst and explosions; vandalism of gas pipelines supplying thermal stations. Other counterproductive acts include the manipulation of the bills to pay less with the arrangement benefiting the bill collector, instead of the nation and the power generating revenue, etc. But frankly, with the seriousness of the energy problem on the nation's survival, these problems do not compare at all. They could be overcome by any administration that is serious enough to tackle it.

The government on its part has the lion share of the responsibility, when it comes to power generation. But successive administrations continue to fail the nation on issues of energy. As much as these governments want us to believe that they are working to find, understand, and address the energy problem, that is bogus. Nations with bigger population and those with less have all been able to supply uninterrupted power to their people. Likewise nations with no such resources for generating electricity have also done it. And you do not even have to look at the developed world; a vast majority of the developing nations also have reliable power supply for their industries and residences.

The energy sector suffers from the same crippling problem as the Nigerian leadership for years, and that is corruption, embezzlement and sheer lack of concern for important issues. The previous democratic administration of Olusegun Obasanjo failed, for example, in its promise to as a priority on taking office, fix the energy problem. After the billions of dollars the administration spent, the problem persists. No one to my knowledge has even been seriously charged, tried and or imprisoned due to such catastrophic level of embezzlement of funds, let alone consider that it was a blatant betrayal of trust when such a project that was at a national crisis level, was neglected, consequently putting us back a decade. It ultimately becomes an issue of hoodwinking the population one again, where commissions get set up later, but no one gets punished even when catastrophic events happen.

One year after the 'Yar Adua administration, a writer Hector Igbikiowubo writing for Vanguard at the one year anniversary of the administration, listed an abysmal state of all power generating facilities of the nation. One problem highlighted was related to gas run thermal stations. Their problem in that regard was that the gas lines supplying feed-stock to thermal power stations were being repeatedly vandalized by militants and aggrieved community youths in the Niger Delta, limiting the power generation capacity of the Power Holding Company of Nigeria, PHCN.

The largest of such thermal stations in the country, Igbikiowubo writes, is Egbin Thermal Power Station, with a rated power generation capacity of 1,320 Megawatts but was reduced to producing an average of 300Mw (a mere quarter of its full capacity). While the 414 Megawatt Geregu Thermal Power Station in Kogi State, the 335Mw Papalanto Thermal Power Station in Ogun State, the 335Mw Omotosho Thermal Power Station in Ondo State have all been largely unproductive owing to acts of vandalism of gas pipelines.

Statistical records indicate that most of the existing industries in the country have back-up power generators because of unreliable and constant power interruptions. These include: the hotels services sub-sector, small and medium scale enterprises, operators in the maritime sector and conglomerates among others. The result is a compounded problem, i.e. over-utilization of an already scarce resource (diesel and gas), as well as the escalation of production costs for industries who have to run mostly on back up generated power at a much higher cost than regular electricity from the grid. The scarcity of the diesel comes from increasing demands from industries; while the nation's refineries are also operating on low fraction capacities due to vandalism and maintenance failures linked mostly to corrupt practices. It's a multi faceted problem.

Investigations conducted last year (2009), according to the vanguard report, revealed that there are about 12,230 power consuming businesses spread across the country with each of them using private power generating sets with installed capacity ranging between 150 and 2000KVH. They averagely consume about 400 liters of diesel per day. That is a total of about 4.9 million liters per day, 151.652 per month or 1.820 billion liters of diesel per annum.

We will urge all administrations to persistently work on alleviating the energy crisis the nation faces, in order to revive as well as generate even more industries. We know it is a bigger task than most, but we caution that it actually does not have to be capital intensive; a way for the wolves to come running only to line their pockets. Concentrate on changing attitudes and also circumventing corruption. Every citizen has been beaten hard enough on issues of reliable power supply, that it should not be a daunting task. The government for example can separate the various aspects of the project by separating the funds, from the designers of the project; the fund holding location from the approval process for its allocation and use. In fact, the office of the President can keep direct tabs on the issue, just as the past administration did to the Petroleum portfolio. That should give the project the attention and importance it deserves.

Chapter Three

The Nigerian Electrical Challenges

Hadiza Wada, DBA

December 19, 2009

Introduction:

Nigeria, a country of about 140 million has been grappling with energy challenges for decades. Various governments and administrations have come and gone, but just a very few have made the energy challenge a priority, and those that have, did not last long enough to make any impact. As could be seen, and as the case is generally in all nations across the world; regardless of who is in power at any given time, there are national priorities that should not and are never compromised no matter what. Energy, as the engine that powers growth, development and prosperity is one of them. The reality however in Nigeria is; only a small percentage of residential requirement of electricity as well as industrial requirement are being met. The average daily supply of electricity in most cities does not exceed eight hours daily (less than 35% daily requirement). In fact the World Bank has reported that 90% of businesses could not rely on electricity supply in Nigeria and have turned to individual and mechanically generated engines (generators) for their power needs, at great costs to themselves and the Nigerian economy.

Present Statistics

70% of Nigerians, mostly living outside of major cities have no access to electricity. This in itself is catastrophic. With a population of about 140 Million, keeping 70% of that amount out of the realms of utilization of electricity to help simplify even simple chores should spell catastrophic consequences to growth, development, and even at times basic survival. It is tantamount to living in the Stone Age where simple tasks take up a lot of time and resources. If a great majority of our rural population have to fetch wood from the forest just to simply boil water for breakfast and take a warm bath every morning as opposed to waking up and heating both in minutes using an electric coil, the human resource wasted must be enormous. And this is just about morning bath and breakfast. What about one's professional requirements even in cities; when he or she steps out of the house to earn a living. Why should anyone, in the 21st century, be denied the simple ability to rely on electricity to light his office, power some simple office equipments that simplify official duties allowing one to communicate with businesses and also official partners across the nation and the world? We are just highlighting simple uses not industrial ones.

The statistics today is that three quarters of the country's population are dependent on wood as fuel for cooking food daily which shows the alarming rate at which deforestation is occurring. Fuel wood accounts for over 50% of overall energy consumption in the country and is the dominant source of energy in the domestic sector (Nigeria Energy Policy 2003). Though not seriously analyzed because most people have come to accept firewood as a fact of life, in actual fact emission from firewood is toxic especially when used indoors. Just as smoking tobacco (leaves) leads to serious health issues; burning firewood (trees) daily and inhaling the smoke is also toxic. As of today the toll of harvesting the forests for firewood has caused mass deforestation in the northern part of the country, and that is the breadbasket of the nation. Deforestation as a result of firewood usage has increased the rate at which desert encroachment has devastated the six Northernmost states of the federation; Borno, Yobe, Jigawa, Katsina, Zamfara and Sokoto (in this order East to West).

The trend of deforestation and desert encroachment especially in the north is currently at a rate of 300,000 Hectares per year. It is actually frightening if you have flown by air across other nations of the world, as opposed to flying across the African continent or its nations. Not only does deforestation for wood takes enormous amounts from the forests, hardly do any of such nations engage in putting back what they have harvested of the natural forests. At the rate of population growth, even if we continue to replace every tree taken down, or even three for each taken down, it will not heal the devastation, as trees take years to grow but a day or less to cut down. Agricultural land is also severely being affected by wood fuel use, causing erosion and rapid degeneration of soil fertility. Finally the overall efficiency of the wood burning process is very low, less that 12%. That means that most of the heat generated is not utilized by the cooking pot, but is dissolved into the air or absorbed by other things not intended to be heated by it.

The impact of unstable or non existent electrical energy for Nigerian Industries is enormous. The primary impact alone (direct), not counting secondary impact such as the loss of employment from private sector industries, is great. Low commercial energy use is correlated with high infant mortality, illiteracy and infertility, and with low life expectancy (UNDP 2000, p. 42). As Nigeria's electrical power generation and distribution dwindles over the years, many industries have been closed permanently, some temporarily in the hope that some miracle from Federal and State Governments that have been asleep for long, may resuscitate them. Just recently the Southern commercial capital of Lagos State has also started crying out owing to the general lack of industrial energy capacity for its teeming industries. For Kano, the Major Northern Nigerian Industrial city, it has been the issue for close to a decade now.

In Kano, some 70% of its industrial capacity has been wiped out by lack of energy. Inflation and lack of market for its ever increasing prices, in addition to importation of cheaper alternatives have forced industries out of production. Energy is one of the major culprits in that regard because for every kilowatt of electricity generated through PHCN at a cost of N6, its alternative in direct diesel costs per generator use is N35, a six times cost per kilowatt hour increase. Well over 90% of businesses in Nigeria today have generators (World Bank, 2005).

Another issue responsible for the closures is lack of coordination in effective local cultivation and utilization of raw materials; and finally faulty export/import governmental policy and implementation. Even in cases where governmental policy supports local industries, overwhelming smuggling in of foreign goods at both land and port entries is at a proportion that demonstrates the sheer lack of patriotism and concern by Nigerians to take charge and help themselves. And for every container of smuggled goods, an equal number of domestically produced products is practically wasted and strangled.

Structural Problems

Presently, Nigeria's main sources of power generation are Gas and Hydro. The Hydro power generation stations at Kainji, Jebba and Shiroro are all performing well below capacity, with most of their turbines being non-operational for long durations. That greatly cuts down their generation capacity. Lower river capacity flow plus lack of maintenance and obsolete generation equipment is responsible. Otherwise it is the most cost effective way forward for the country and the world. It does not emit environmental pollutants as gas and coal do, and it is powered by natural flowing water (no additional costs).

Hydropower converts the energy within the force of flowing water into electricity. The quantity of electricity generated is determined by the volume of water flow and the amount of "head" (the height from the turbine outlet to the water surface at the lower level of the river) after the water passes through the turbines. The greater the flow towards the turbines, and head (the height of the drop in meters), the more electricity produced. If adequately harnessed, it is the most fitting source for Nigeria for many reasons. Hydropower is a clean, a domestic and renewable source of energy. Hydropower plants provide inexpensive electricity and produce no pollution like ones powered by gas. And, unlike other energy sources such as those powered by gas, water is not destroyed during the production of electricity—it can be reused for other purposes, such as irrigation.

Kainji Dam extends for about 10 km (about 6 mi), including its saddle dam, which closes off a tributary valley. The center section, housing the hydroelectric turbines, was built from concrete. This section is 65 m (215 ft) high. The dam was designed to have a generating capacity of 960 Megawatts; however, only 10 of its 12 turbines have been installed, reducing the capacity to 800 Megawatts. Of the 10, only a fraction (4-2) have been working for years.

Hydro Elec. Station	Capacity	Year completed	Reservoir	River
Kianji	800MW	1968	Kianji Lake	Niger River
Jebba	540MW	1985	Lake Jebba	Niger
Shiroro	600MW	1990	Lake Shiroro	Kaduna River
Kano	100MW	2015		Hadejia River
Zamfara	100MW	2012	Gotowa	Bunsuru River
Kiri Power	35MW	2016		Benue River

Courtesy Wikipedia, the free encyclopedia.

To further complicate the small percentage of the generated power versus capacity produced by the three major hydro electricity power plants, about 35% to 45% of generated electricity is lost in transmission due to theft, and lack of modern equipment among other things. Another problem is lack of qualified staff and over staffing of mediocre ones to manage the facilities available. Qualified staffs do exist within the country but nepotism and corruption has not allowed them the opportunity to be engaged in managing and taking care of the facilities. Nigeria's energy demand is estimated at 10,000MW, but the installed capacity is about 6000MW and the present operating capacity is reported as less than 2000MW. Water flow problems and obsolete equipment has undermined the three major hydro stations (Kainji, Jebba and Shiroro). The three upcoming hydro stations (above) have a later inception date ranging from three to seven years with an additional capacity of 235 megawatts of locally (state) produced and consumed power.

The Gas generated plants have also been overwhelmed by different brands of problems. The main problem rests with non-patriotic and self indulged citizens. There are five thermal stations located at Afam, Sapele, Egbin, Ughelli and Ijora, all in Southern Nigeria (with a combined installed capacity of 3,976 mega watts). The gas generated energy plants suffer from incessant gas pipelines attacks which continue to disrupt gas supplies to the power stations. Those responsible for the disruptions have been credibly reported by both Nigerian internal and also foreign external sources as having strong connections and backing from local state governors in their areas. Other sources report the militant's use by external market forces to play demand supply games that increases the volatility as well as speculative oil marketing in world financial markets.

Such disruptions and especially the sabotage involving pipelines have also caused the closure of two major refineries in Nigeria, further constricting the refining capacity of the nation in vehicular as well as industrial gas production capacities. The disruptions have cut refining capacity by 50%. The refineries in Kaduna and Warri are virtually closed, which forced the nation that produces manifold oil than it needs for internal consumption to start importing refined oil and its corresponding products from other countries. The two refineries of Warri and Kaduna refine roughly half of total refined products at 110,000 and 125,000 barrels per day each, as compared to the combined Port Harcourt refinery I and II that have the capacity to refine the remaining 50% at about a quarter of a million barrels a day (Mbendi information Services). Such is the impact on the gas powered generating plants on one hand, and the industries that rely on refined diesel gas in lieu of the absence of electricity on the other. The impact is enormous.

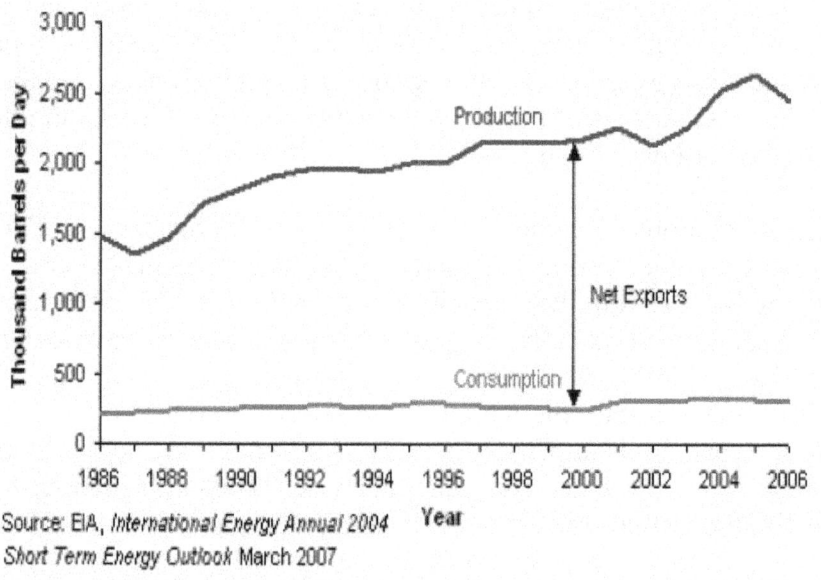

Production (top), Internal Consumption (bottom), 1986-2006. The difference (vertical line) is exported.

Refinement Challenges

Nigeria has three refineries, all owned by the Nigerian National Petroleum Company, NNPC. The oil refineries convert crude oil into fuel products, lubricating oils, bitumen and chemical feedstock. The Nigerian government has announced its intention to sell 51% of each of the refineries to private investors in 2004. **(a)** The Kaduna refinery in northern Nigeria was built in 1980 with a capacity of 5.5 million metric tons per year (mt/yr), or 110,000 barrel per day (b/d). A Lube Base oil plant was added in 1982 and a LAB plant in 1987. **(b)** The Warri refinery in the South Central region was built in 1978 with a capacity of 6.2 million mt/yr (125,000 b/d). A Carbon Black plant and a Polypropylene plant were added in 1986. **(c)** The Port Harcourt refinery in the southeast is made up of two refineries, built in 1965 and 1989. In

1993 they were merged into one, with a total capacity of 10.500 million mt/yr (210,000 b/d). The Eleme Petrochemical plant, which was built adjacent to the Port Harcourt refinery in 1995, has a production capacity of 483,000 mt/yr, a Polypropylene capacity of 80,000 mt/yr, and a Polyethylene production capacity of 250,000 mt/yr.

As mentioned earlier on, Nigeria's energy demand is estimated at 10,000MW, the installed capacity 6000MW and the present operating capacity is less than 2000MW. Furthermore, the maximum transmission grid capacity is just 4000MW even when generation is expected to rise beyond that. That literally means unless the capacity is updated and upgraded (increased) you cannot use the present structure to store or distribute the higher generated electrical power. Zoning issues and illegal connections also contribute to the poor grid. By overloading the capacity built into regional transformers through illegal connections and the subsequent increase in demand from them, the transformers consequently fail or burst. Poorly planned and executed rural electrification projects by various state governments have also been cited for causing overload (increased demand) on the grid thereby reducing reliability. There is also unpatriotic and criminal sabotage to the grid, including stealing of power cables and transmission accessories; another crucial structural dilemma affecting the grid.

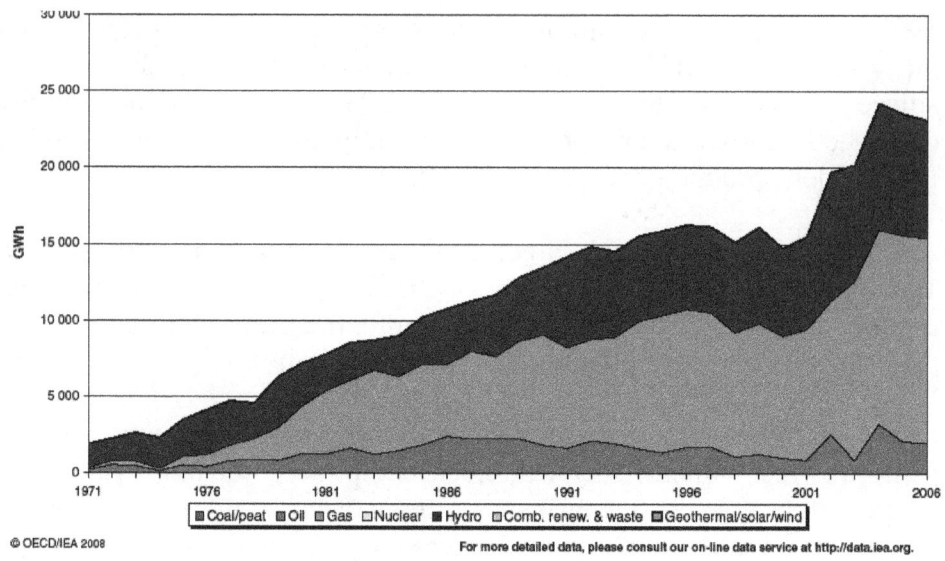

Nigerian Electrical generation capacity, top Hydro, then Gas (middle) and Oil (bottom), in gigawatt per hour. *Courtesy of International Energy Agency, IEA*

Presently as per statistical representation of electrical generation in Nigeria recorded with the International Energy Agency, the three main sources of electrical power are segmented as represented by the graph above. The sources are Hydro, Gas and Oil.

Unutilized Natural Gas Potential

Nigeria has the 7th largest gas reserves in the world, but it is presently unutilized. Since about half a decade ago, Nigeria has been flaring 2.6 bcf/day of its natural gas, a 12.5% total of all globally flared gas and an equivalent to 30% of European Union's annual gas consumption. This has been largely viewed as not only irresponsible in monetary terms, but environmentally deplorable. It is acceptable to assume the developed nations with the ability to assist the nation build modern means of harnessing and delivering such gas may not be readily helpful giving international competition vis-à-vis corporate industrial maneuvers,

Nigeria should actually blame itself for not being able to work out even a mutually beneficial arrangement with willing nations.

It could be recalled that the Murtadha/Obasanjo military administration in an unprecedented move nationalized the Nigerian Oil Sector and set a very ambitious plan to develop and profit from the venture in general, a move widely criticized and challenged by the multinational corporations. These multinational corporations were at that time the major profiteers from Nigerian oil exploration, drilling, shipment and refinement. They were readily engaged in gas flaring without recourse to the monetary loss, and environmental degradation that it causes.

In a direct discussion with this writer in 2005, a Nigerian former Head of State, General Muhammadu Buhari who was the Petroleum Minister for Nigeria from the Murtadha Administration until its civilian handover of power to the Shagari Administration in 1979, expressed his highest regrets over the reluctance of the Shagari Administration with its unwillingness to go ahead and implement the agreement for harnessing liquefied natural gas (Liquefied Natural Gas Project) LNGP, worked out by the previous administration.

The Shagari administration refused to implement the project, as various news sources opined at that time that the officials of the administration received bribes from Multinational Corporations to literally sit tight on the project. Later when Buhari got the chance to rule the nation, he revived and tried to implement the LNGP, but that administration again was short lived. The Babangida Administration that replaced Buhari's decided to put the final nail to the coffin. Had it gone ahead as planned, General Buhari opined, Nigeria would have been not only much more prosperous, it could have provided the opportunity to develop the whole region. The Murtala vision, revived just for a short while by his oil Minister Buhari during the latter's regime, was to free Nigerian oil resource for Nigerians, just as other nations of the OPEC cartel such as Saudi Arabia, Iraq and more did at about the same time, including Venezuela and are now enjoying that prosperity.

The Energy sector is further handicapped by endemic corruption. NIPP projects launched with capital outlay of $9.7 billion to increase power output by around 2744MW expand transmission and distribution network has its own problems. The projects have serious deficiencies; faulty procurement and sequencing of contracts, poor planning, logistics and weak management. Most of the NIPPs projects are located in the most volatile region of Niger Delta, another inbuilt misjudgment. Recent power contract investigations by the national assembly also illustrate what is clearly wrong with Nigeria. With no dam of its own or the corresponding river to make one, many shipped equipments including the Obasanjo Administration procured turbines from General Electric, still lay waste in the port city of Lagos, and have not been moved to the location they were meant for. In short the project wasted billions in dollar terms and has not benefited the nation in any percentage terms or capacity to date.

Results and recommendations

Nigeria's dream of being among the top 20 developed nations will remain just a dream unless it solves its energy problems. Failure to consider the role of energy in supporting the efforts to reach the Millennium Development Goals (MDGs) is undermining the development options pursued, the poverty reduction targets, and the effectiveness of resources invested. It is true that access to energy is critical to achieving virtually all the MDG's & Vision 2020. This is partially because energy consumption is highly correlated with higher GDP per capita of every nation. Nigeria's energy crisis limits the opportunities to bring its citizens out of poverty. In 1980 for example, only 28% was considered poor, yet today 71% of the population is reported to live on less than one dollar a day.

The data above all tend to point to a need for serious and responsible coordination of coherent and comprehensive energy policy for the country. There is a need to draw a blue print for their sustainable development, supply and utilization of energy resources within the economy, and for the use of such resources in international trade and co-operation. It is reported that a 2003 energy policy document is in place, but no framework for its implementation has yet been marked out.

Another glaring problem discussed for decades without taking any action revolves around the fact that energy infrastructure is mainly owned by the Federal Government. It is not by itself a problem, as long as the ability to generate and coordinate power usage by state governments are available, and taken seriously by the state and local governments across the nation. Civilian governments with state assemblies are empowered by the constitution to seek unique solutions to any of their unique problems. Such issues therefore need to be taken up and coordinated well.

The State governments have not taken it upon themselves to find alternative sources to generate power for its population's unique residential and industrial requirements. In the early sixties for example, the Benue-Plateau government was still using the independent regional (Kuru Falls) power generation facility (NESCO) built initially to power mining activities by the mining companies during colonial administration. It was for long after independence used to provide all electrical needs of at least three major metropolitan areas including the capital city of Jos.

The National Electricity Supply Company (NESCO) as it was then called was reported to be generating and supplying about 19 MW, at a time when the federal counterpart was named Electric Corporation of Nigeria ECN supplying power to the nation. So harnessing independent power sources is not a policy unheard of, it was a state level policy that has worked in the past. Energy decisions need to be coordinated at all levels of government, local, state, and federal. At present local and state governments are not fully involved in solving the crisis in their domains directly. Most states however have both the financial and natural resources to independently provide for their populations for growth and prosperity.

In other areas of the country the challenges are geographical (UNIDO, 2006). States can make a difference with such challenges, by investing and reaping the benefits directly, as well as helping develop their communities. It is reported that roughly 60% of households in mangrove areas of the South are yet to get access to electricity because of the difficulty in drawing electric lines through the forest areas. In these areas stand-alone Small Hydro Power stations are an alternative (simple and economically viable).

The many advantages of such decentralized hydro arrangements are: "1. Can defer/avoid expenditure on long transmission and distribution network. 2. Can provide power more quickly to un-serviced areas. 3. Smaller generation options reduce risks for utilities. 4. Can match demand and supply of isolated human communities. 5. Smaller technologies are much less disruptive in terms of population displacement and biophysical effects and can present a more aesthetically and environmentally acceptable alternative to large scale facilities, which are uneconomic in view of low power intensity demanded. 6. Decentralized systems can develop the demand for electricity over time to the point where a grid connection becomes economically feasible."

Additionally, flaring of liquefied natural gas has to be stopped now, and one effective way is to impose fines on oil companies. Meaningful pressure has to be placed on such corporations. Just recently, Nigerian papers reported the unwillingness of national authorities to impose such fines, though past practice has helped in moving forward the LNGP. The Guardian in an Editorial December 14, 2009 reported "...last week when the Minister of State for Petroleum Resources, Odein Ajumogobia, disparaged the entire gas flare-out proposals. He has come up with a well-worn argument of the oil companies, that it is not possible to produce crude oil without burning associated gas. He (proposed) a flare-out date of December 31, 2010." That is sheer irresponsibility, as the paper also seems to indicate. The Buhari Administration since the eighties has imposed fines, and it seemed to have worked, though at first it was widely criticized. The multinational corporations will of course bully and terrorize the authorities concerned, but it is left for them to act in the best interest of the nation, its people, and the environment, and if unable or unwilling, then resign. The authorities today should be pressured to forgo bribes and intimidation by such corporations.

Finally, reforestation has to be taken seriously to replenish depleting forests cut down for domestic fuel uses. There are no fast rules cast in stone that narrows employment to a physically confining office job. Nothing prohibits states and local governments from putting the millions of unemployed youths to work, by assigning to them (with close supervision and adequate pay) hectares of land to plant and care for the much needed trees to arrest desertification, provide shelter against erosion, support agriculture and also provide edible fruits and animal fodder. Planting useful trees such as oranges, mango, cashews, locust bean (*kalwa*), baobab (*kuka*), fig (*baure*), Plum (*tsada*), Acacia and Magarya (used as fodder) and many others already naturally acclimated to the region becomes a doubly useful venture. And it should not be a political point scoring venture that dies after planting with no provision for long term care, or else a project that dies off after the initiator leaves office.

Chapter Four

Nigeria's Forgotten Heroes: Lessons Lost?

Honoring A True Gentleman (Sa'ad Zungur 1915 - 1958)

Though we have many role models in leadership and service in Nigeria, we will feature just two of them: Sa'ad Zungur and Murtala (Murtadha) Muhammed, because in our opinion they have been grossly underrated today, and have almost been forgotten.

Sa'ad Zungur was born into a noble family of Islamic scholars. His family held and I believe still hold the Imam position for the Bauchi Central Mosque. Though a man of deep Islamic scholarship, he was a smart and hard working student and the first Northerner to study Pharmacy, according to Malam Aminu Kano, his political student. Despite his humility, self sacrifice and unmaterialistic personality, Sa'adu was also described by Malam Aminu Kano as a man who fears no one.

Born in November 1913 at Ganjuwa ward of Bauchi city (some sources say 1915), Ahmad Mahmud Sa'ad Zungur, popularly known as "Sa'adu" completed his early education in Bauchi, and proceeded to Katsina for teacher's training. He later attended the Kano School of Hygiene and also Royal School of Hygiene with matriculation in London, England. He graduated with distinction.

The influence of his scholarly family and the knowledge he acquired early, influenced his life significantly. His father Muhammad Bello spoke not only the local city language Hausa, but also Fulfulde (a regional language of cattle herders of West Africa) and Arabic fluently. Gifted with something of photographic memory, Sa'ad was described as a brilliant student of Quranic interpretation (Tafsir), grammar (Nahw), Jurisprudence (Fiqh) and theology, and had a great appetite for learning. Mallam Salman, a cousin of Sa'ad, once told this writer that Sa'ad thinks and ponders a lot over issues, and the family was concerned that he would always be either reading, writing or in deep thought. He has a favorite tree in Zungur, a Giginya tree (an unusually tall tree of the date palm family), where he would sit to contemplate.

He used both his formal (Western) and religious knowledge to confront the wrongs in his society. With his Western education, he became the thorn in the flesh of the British colonial administration, to the extent that they practically banned everyone from giving him an employment. At that time, an employment ban by the colonial administrator practically means a hopeless unemployment situation, as there was virtually no "private sector." Zungur was not deterred. It was later that he formed the first political forum for northern youths and grown ups ever recorded up north. He not only initiated activism against foreign control, he led it with a lot of courage and resolve. His greatest assets were his intellectual gift, and his writings.

Sa'adu's unrelenting campaign was felt on the social level. He campaigned against practices he saw as hindrances to social and economic development. He fought hard against the injustices meted on the general population by local African leadership. Some of the problems were devoid of colonial administration's influence and some he saw as resulting from the local leadership's connivance with colonial administration against the general interest of the nation and its people. In this arena, he used his Islamic knowledge base to attack what he described as injustice and tyranny. Among the common themes he addressed was the growing passiveness and insensitivity to matters of social justice and governance, sold to the community as "respect for leaders."

Writing in August of 1954 for example in relation to a permit sought for a political rally, Sa'adu's letter to the City's leadership council reads:

"NEPU (a political party) in Bauchi will support competent people whom it sees as sincerely committed to promoting the rights and welfare of the people of Bauchi. NEPU would care less about their organizational affiliation or place of origin. The only condition they would satisfy is competence and commitment to honestly improving the welfare of the people."

Though an effective campaigner for social justice, Sa'adu's mode of operation however, was not devoid of respect for his elders and leadership. He was assertive, and appears never to give up on what he believes to be right. He would continue to follow that path until he obtained success in the most peaceful way he could. He was assertive without being unduly rash and disrespectful. An example of this is displayed in the following letter also written to the Bauchi Native Authority Council in April 1956.

> *"We take courage to renew our faith in, and to demonstrate our unflinching loyalty to the Bauchi Native Authority in spite and despite the mortal injury inflicted on our traditional political faith by the recent attitude of the Native Authority towards our progressive political organization NEPU, and its youth wing RSS. Although such attitude has not affected our loyalty to the established authority. We were however extremely disappointed."*

Sa'adu was genuinely a man ahead of his time. In a speech he gave at Kaduna in 1948, twelve years before the realization of Nigerian Independence from colonial rule, Sa'adu described the situation before the nation. He drew analogies to wake the people up from their slumber, that self-government by any name is way ahead of a vote for control by foreigners in one's land.

In presenting his ideas at Kaduna, Sa'adu drew the analogy of the propaganda that fanned slavery, where the European establishments were telling the world that the "negro was not educatable, because he was not a complete human being." And now, he said, to maintain a grip on their colonies in Africa they are telling the world that African colonies are not ready to govern themselves. If anyone should buy that ridiculous idea, he suggested, it should not be the African themselves.

Sa'adu demanded a government which should be sensitive to and answer to the people living on the land, not one that should answer to a foreign government situated thousands of miles across the ocean. At an honorary event in Kano to honor Zungur's contribution to Northern Political awareness, Professor Dandatti Abdulkadir was quoted by the *Daily Triumph* praising the vision of the man, also attributing to Sa'ad Zungur "The initiator of the first Northern Political Party."

As for the need to establish achievable goals people will love as a target of the struggle, Sa'adu described how among any group of people, the good and the bad exist. Among the imperialists living on African land, there were a few officers sent by the imperial government who saw the reality of the nature of the average African as sensitive, hospitable and embodying every other virtue there was anywhere else in the world. Likewise among the activists for freedom, there were those who do not have any genuine interest for freedom, either out of weakness, or greed. Africans with such self-defeating attitude he described were the ones that are usually used to deter other Africans with genuine interest in freedom.

Sa'adu was a writer, who did not relent until he breathed his last. His appeal across religious and ethnic lines provided him with opportunities to write columns, articles, and serialized publications for both Northern and Southern publications. He described himself as a thinker whose faculties for thought and expression were out of his control. He believed it was his calling to live for justice and spread it as far and as wide as he could. His passion for writing instead of speaking, he says, is borne out of his ill-health on the one hand, and also his personality of humility and soft speech. In his own words to the Bauchi Divisional Officer

"I prefer to write rather than speak. If I sit in a place with you I am sure to be overpowered by your personality; and I must out of obedience and politeness listens more and speak less. I write because I feel these things so passionately that I must cry out. I have tried not to write this letter. I tried to put the thought of the destiny of Northern Nigeria behind me...I cannot. I go to bed with these thoughts; I get up with them."

Sa'adu suffered from a suspicious undiagnosed ailment that some later described as possibly asthma, others as tuberculosis. Being a thorn in the sides of both colonial and local leadership in his struggle for justice and fair treatment of his fellow beings, no one bothered to provide adequate treatment. And he remained unemployed for a greater part of his adult life; most of the services he provided were voluntary and free. He offered free service wherever he got the chance, and later succumbed to his ailment in his midlife.

General Murtadha Muhammad

Head of State July 30, 1975 – February 13, 1976

Introduction

Murtadha (b. November 8, 1938 – d. February 13, 1976) was one of the most promising of all the Head of States that Nigeria ever saw. He stands alone in various categories of leadership effectiveness. Murtadha was also unparalleled in motivating towards productivity, ridding the nation of corruption, redefining Nigerian Foreign Policy goals, and a host of other remarkable and laudable ideals, which we will list shortly. Personality wise, he was very practical and pragmatic. *(Picture courtesy of Wikipedia, Murtala left, and Bolaji Akinyemi)*

His destiny appears to have been charted out boldly for him, taking him from formal military studies, training, and practice in both the Nigerian civil war and Peacekeeping operation in the Congo, finally back to face his destiny, ruling the nation. Having participated visibly and courageously in the Nigerian Civil War you would of course find some very critical accounts of his service, especially seeing that Civil wars do not usually make uncontested heroes or a vanquished lot. But no objective individual who witnessed his performance first hand will deny him his hard earned credit.

To understand military disruptions of civilian administrations, one has to understand the history behind it. Having gained its independence from British colonial control on the first day of October 1960, Nigeria began its journey of self government experimenting first with the British Parliamentary System. Shortly after the second elections that brought back the Nigerian People's Congress (NPC) for a second term under the leadership of Sir Abubakar Tafawa Balewa as Prime Minister, in January 1966, some rebellious officers of the army mostly of the South Eastern Nigeria's ethnic Igbo, staged a coup where Northern Muslim leaders were almost exclusively killed. The Prime Minister living at the Capital of Lagos, plus the Northern Regional Administrator, also Chair of the Ruling Party, Sir Ahmadu Bello were murdered. The Prime Minister was first abducted to the suburbs and gruesomely executed, while Premier Ahmadu Bello was shot at his residence in Kaduna, up North.

Many analysts have opined that had the military administration that took over brought justice to bear on those who disrupted the government and committed those heinous and gruesome murders; the history of Nigeria might have taken a different course. Delayed justice has been proven to lead to catastrophic consequences in history. To make matters worse, the high ranking Army Officer who persuaded (some sources say ordered) the civilians to relinquish the reigns of power to him, Major General Aguyi Ironsi, is of the same ethnic, regional, and religious affiliation with the coup executors and murderers of Nigerian Leaders.

Even if the country was to assume that Major General Ironsi, was not part of the scheme or had wind of it, his attitude and actions afterwards displayed in unambiguous terms to Nigerians that he was not going to punish anyone. That inaction lasted from January 1966 to July 1966. Tension has never subsided since the murders. Pressure and counsel from centuries old traditional institutions of the North comprising of Emirs, Judges, Scholars and elders who saw the coup, the killings, and the prevailing order that replaced it as an affront with the potential to explode, was not heeded by the Ironsi military government.

Soon rebellion against General Ironsi and his officers erupted in July 1966, with a countercoup that saw Ironsi and his right hand man Colonel Adekunle Fajuyi, the Western Region's first Military Administrator killed. The mutiny by Northern military officers started probably as a last straw for Northern leaders and army personnel, who felt they have waited enough for justice that has not materialized, while they continue to be further victimized by insensitive cartoons of their slain leaders and insults from Southern dominated press. The coup started the same night Major General Ironsi concluded a meeting with Nigerian Traditional rulers as the guests of Col Fajuyi.

The nation chose a young Army Lieutenant Colonel Yakubu Gowon to lead. He was a compromise choice, which was critical at that time, because he was a Northerner but a Christian. His temperament was also sometimes brought up as one of the qualities that made him a wise choice, which his counterparts saw as required for negotiating the nation's way out of its prevailing tense circumstance.

But after exactly nine years, overseeing the country through the war years, the Gowon Administration was also overthrown in a first ever bloodless coup, arranged to coincide with his trip to Uganda to attend the Organization of African Unity summit in July of 1975. His government has gradually become unpopular, with allegations of corruption, ineptitude, and growing insensitivity to Nigeria's problems. The Army, a branch that produced the Head of State was disillusioned by the performance of one of them, which seemed to make a mockery of what they have fought with great sacrifice to instill and ensure its success. Details of the reasons were described in the next leader's first speech to the nation, one day after the coup on July 30, 1975. That leader was Brigadier Murtala Muhammed *(See a copy of speech at the conclusion of this topic).*

After a series of close door meetings, during which all the nation's broadcast stations were airing no other broadcasts but martial music with brief interruptions of news bulletins about the situation, the announcement came on air that Brigadier Murtala Muhammed will be the next Head of State. On how he got there, Ammani in his tribute to Murtala in 2009 described that those who executed the coup first offered the position to Brigadier Muhammed, but he would not take it, so they offered it to Brigadier T. Y. Danjuma and Brigadier Olusegun Obasanjo, both of whom declined and counsel them to persuade Brigadier Murtala, being the best choice for that time and occasion.

Gen Murtala Rahmat Muhammed Tribute.

Aliyu Ammani

February 13, 2010

The article was first written for publication at last year's anniversary February 2009, and does more justice to the Late Murtala, in the Publisher's opinion, than most reviewed; it is run in its entirety here.

Throughout the world and across all ages and climes, there have been a handful of outstanding personalities who have left their marks indelibly in the sands of history of the lands and nations in which they have lived. These were the heroes who sacrificed tremendously to change the course of history among their peoples.

The communities that constitute today's Nigeria have each its own heroes. At the national arena, most of those we referred to as our heroes have fallen victims of what I called *the Zik Syndrome*, what Kole Omotosho described as a repeat of Zik of Africa, Zik of Nigeria, Zik of Eastern Region, Zik of Onitsha and finally ordinary Zik. Put on a pedestal was General Murtala Rahmat Muhammed, our national, nay African hero.

General Yakubu Gowon fought to keep Nigeria one. Some of us can still recall his war slogan: *To Keep Nigeria One is a Task that Must be Done*. He would have been our version of Abraham Lincoln, but for the fact that he overstayed his welcome. The civil war hero Yakubu Gowon's administration of Nigeria was characterized by what Nigerians believed to be inertia, lethargy, corruption and decadence. The last straw that broke the camel's back was that Gowon reneged on his 1970 promise to return the nation to democratic rule in 1976, describing the date as unrealistic, that 6 years was too short a period for his Military Government to accomplish its reconstruction program and preparation for return to democratic rule.

On Tuesday the 29th of July 1975 the Military struck for the third time in our nation's history. The inept administration of General Gowon was toppled in a mercifully bloodless coup, the first in our nation's history of military incursion in politics. The task of cleansing the Augean stable rested on the shoulders of Brigadier Murtala Ramat Muhammed. Thus began, the 199 most dynamic, pragmatic, breathtaking, purpose driven, result oriented period of our country's political history.

The 13th day of February 2010 marked exactly 34 years from the very day some disgruntled elements within the Nigerian Armed Forces murdered, in cold blood, General Murtala Muhammed in an attempt to take over power. Never in the history of Nigeria was any Nigerian mourned by the totality of Nigerians as was General Murtala. His death was an intensely and intimately felt national loss. Though the coup plotters succeeded in snuffing out the flame, the coup was abortive. The rest is history.

This write-up is an attempt to commemorate the death and immortality of General Murtala Rahmat Muhammed, the dynamism of his 199 days leadership of the Nigerian nation, what was referred to as the 200 Days of *Ramatism*.

Brigadier Murtala Rahmat Muhammad had not wanted to be Head of State. But he had been the choice of the coup plotters known then as *the Junta*, since the day in April when a few of them, distraught over the state of the country, began to conceive the idea of the coup. When after the successful completion of the coup on the 29th of July 1975, *the Junta* leaders: Colonels Joe Garba, Abdullahi Mohammed and Shehu 'Yar Adua offered the leadership of the Nigerian nation to Murtala, he burst out "To hell with you! I have said I don't want to be anybody's Head of State". Murtala was the ace of the ruling triumvirate proposed by *the Junta*, and when he declined their offer, they offered the leadership first to Brigadier Obasanjo and then to Brigadier T. Y. Danjuma, but both declined; supporting Murtala as the obvious choice and imploring *the Junta* to do all they could to persuade him. When Murtala finally accepted to be Head of State, nobody then knew that he was making a pact with history and destiny to make the supreme sacrifice for the Nigerian nation 199 days later.

Murtala jolted a sleeping nation into life. The vibrancy in his voice was arresting. The fire in his eyes charmed and awed the nation. In contrast to the extravagant style of Gowon, Murtala adopted a low profile policy.

The 504 replaced Mercedes Benz as the official government car. Only the Head of State rode a Mercedes Benz: not bullet proof and not the 600 series type.

For the 200 days Murtala was Head of State, he lived in the house he had occupied as Director of Army Signal Corps. He drove to work at the Dodan Barracks every morning from his house accompanied by his driver, his orderly and his ADC. No convoy. No sirens. No outriders. Few days after his assumption of office, Murtala shunned the sirens and convoy and rode alone with his driver, from Lagos to Kano, a journey of more than one thousand kilometers, in his personal car.

Murtala had never detained a single person in the six months that he led the Nigerian nation. When former Lagos University Law Lecturer Dr. Obarogie Ohonbamu wrote in his magazine *African Spark* that Murtala had corruptly enriched himself before becoming Head of State, and accused him of owing fleets of trailers and rows of houses; Murtala did not descend on him with his heavy boot as most military dictators, he quietly went to Igbosere magistrate court and sued Ohonbamu for libel. The then Federal Director of Public Prosecution on behalf of the Attorney General of the federation promised that Ohonbanu would be given "every reasonable opportunity to prove or justify his assertion" including "freedom of the (entire) country of Nigeria to enable him search for and obtain his proof" because "we do not intend to muzzle anyone. The whole nation was interested in the validity of the assertion complained of." At the last hearing, the case was adjourned till the 17th of March 1976. Murtala was assassinated on the 13th of February.

In an interview with *The Punch* of May 4th 1982, the late Chief MKO Abiola, a very close friend of Murtala, said that Murtala had only seven naira twenty-two kobo (N7.22) in his bank account when he died.

To repudiate the accommodation of bad conduct by the Gowon's administration and to strengthen the civil service, Murtala embarked on the purges that were considered as a great show of bravado. About 10,000 civil servants were dismissed or retired on grounds of corruption, indolence, redundancy, declining productivity or health.

To wipe out emotional attachments to the regions of the first republic and foster national unity, Murtala not only took over the then regionally owned Universities of Ife and that of Ahmadu Bello in Zaria, but also declared that "States will no longer be described by reference to geographical points such as North and South, East or West." Thus the then North Central became the old Kaduna State, Mid West became the old Bendel State and South Eastern State became the old Cross River State.

Panels were set up, and their findings and recommendations put to meaningful use. Murtala created 7 new states bringing the number to 19 following the acceptance of the Justice Ayo Irikefe Panel to examine the agitation for more states. The new Federal Capital Authority Abuja was also created, following the acceptance of the Akinola Aguda Panel.

Murtala in his only Independence Day broadcast enunciated an ambitious five-stage political program that ushered in democratic rule by October 1979. On the 18th of October 1975, Murtala set-up the Constitution Drafting Committee, to fashion out a constitution for Nigeria. In the view of *West Africa*, a regional magazine, "Never in the history of Africa have so many people been consulted so thoroughly about how they wished to be governed." Credit must be given to General Olusegun Obasanjo for the faithfulness and courage with which he successfully executed the concrete and meaningful program that General Murtala mapped out for Nigeria.

Murtala pursued an aggressive foreign policy with Africa as its centre piece. He made it clear to Colonel Joe Garba, his foreign Minister, that he wanted a very activist foreign policy. Nigeria, he said, must be visible in the world. Murtala demonstrated a radical impulse in foreign policy. His message to the close of the Ghana-Nigeria Games held in Accra in the August of 1975 reads "Any glib talk about African unity does not mean much if the desire is not subjected to test."

On the 11th of January 1976, an extra-ordinary meeting of the OAU heads of Government was convened to tackle the Angolan question. Initially, Murtala showed little interest in attending the conference; Obasanjo his Chief of Staff Supreme Headquarters was making preparations to make an appearance in his place. Suddenly an event happened that made him changed his mind and compelled him to make the historic and flamboyant appearance at the conference where he gave the powerful *Africa has come of Age* speech; and this is what happened.

On the 3rd of January 1976, the American Ambassador to Nigeria, Mr. Donald Easum, brought a letter addressed to the Nigerian Head of State from the United States President Gerald Ford. The same letter was sent to many African leaders. Murtala was furious about the content. As a consequence, not only did the Federal Military Government take the bold and unprecedented step of releasing President Ford's letter to the press, it also issued a strong response to it later that evening calling it a "gross insult" and in sum, telling the Americans to go to hell. This event triggered Murtala's decision to attend the conference and deliver his message to the world.

"Mr. Chairman, when I contemplate the evils of apartheid, my heart bleeds and I am sure the heart of every true blooded African bleeds." Thus, Murtala opened the powerful and deep moving *Africa has come of Age* speech. "Rather than join hands with the forces fighting for self-determination and against racism and apartheid, the United States policy makers clearly decided that it was in the best interests of their country to maintain white supremacy and minority regimes in Africa ... Africa has come of age. It's no longer under the orbit of any extra continental power. It should no longer take orders from any country no matter how powerful... gone are the days when Africa will ever bow to the threat of any so-called superpower..." There was thunderous ovation from the Africa Hall and Murtala Muhammed went back to his seat, little knowing that he had exactly 34 days more to live.

Murtala's forceful delivery of an already tough speech literally grounded the anti MPLA forces. He engaged himself in visiting and lobbying other heads of state to support the MPLA. According to Joe Garba, Murtala daily chalked up in his office the number of the countries Nigeria converted to the MPLA side. Murtala's support for the MPLA, which not only USA and Britain were fiercely opposing but even the Saudi government was opposing by funding the FNLA, goes a long way to show Murtala's bold, decisive and patriotic stand on Southern Africa. "Murtala established very forcefully" wrote Patrick Wilmot "that the fight was between African Nationalism, the right of the Blackman to freedom, and Western Imperialism… There was no question of Apartheid South Africa fighting the political red herring of 'International Communism.'

Murtala was a military leader who did not seize power himself, but was invited, by the coup makers, to lead the Federal Military Government, because of the confidence they had in him being the most suitable to give Nigeria the dynamic, purposeful and efficient leadership it required. Nigerians identified with Murtala because he did what he said he came to do and much more. His bold, assertive, proactive leadership gave Nigerians a sense of belonging, hope and strength in the Nigeria project. Like the twinkle of a star, General Murtala Rahmat Muhammed entered and departed the Nigerian, African nay world's political arena. The impact of his charismatic and dynamic leadership permeates every facet of the Nigerian nation. The name Murtala will be with us forever.

First Address to the Nation, July 30 1975

Fellow Nigerians: Events of the past few years have indicated that despite our great human and material resources, the Government has not been able to fulfill the legitimate expectations of our people. Nigeria has been left to drift. This situation, if not arrested, would inevitably have resulted in chaos and even bloodshed. In the endeavor to build a strong, united and virile nation, Nigerians have shed much blood. The thought of further bloodshed, for whatever reasons must, I am sure, be revolting to our people. The Armed Forces, having examined the situation, came to the conclusion that certain changes were inevitable.

After the civil war, the affairs of state, hitherto a collective responsibility became characterized by lack of consultation, indecision, indiscipline and even neglect. Indeed, the public at large became disillusioned and disappointed by these developments. This trend was clearly incompatible with the philosophy and image of a corrective regime. Unknown to the general public, the feeling of disillusionment was also evident among members of the armed forces whose administration was neglected but who, out of sheer loyalty to the Nation, and in the hope that there would be a change, continued to suffer in silence.

Things got to a stage where the head of administration became virtually inaccessible even to official advisers; and when advice was tendered, it was often ignored. Responsible opinion, including advice by eminent Nigerians, traditional rulers, intellectuals, et cetera, was similarly discarded. The leadership, either by design or default, had become too insensitive to the true feelings and yearnings of the people. The nation was thus plunged inexorably into chaos.

It was obvious that matters could not, and should not, be allowed in this manner, and in order to give the nation a new lease of life, and sense of direction, the following decisions were taken:

1. The removal of General Yakubu Gowon as Head of the Federal Military Government and Commander in Chief of the Armed Forces.

2. The retirement of General Yakubu Gowon from the Armed Forces in his present rank of General with full benefits, in recognition of his past services to the nation.

3. General Gowon will be free to return to the country as soon as conditions permit; he will be free to pursue any legitimate undertakings of his choice in any part of the country. His personal safety and freedom and those of his family will be guaranteed.

4. The following members of the Armed Forces are retired with immediate effect:

Vice Admiral JEA Wey - Chief of Staff, Supreme HQ,
Major-General Hassan Katsina - Deputy Chief of Staff, Supreme HQ,
Major-General David Ejoor - Chief of Staff(Army),
Rear Admiral Nelson Soroh - Chief of Naval Staff,
Brigadier EE Ikwue - Chief of Air Staff, and
all other officers of the rank of major general (or equivalent) and above.

Alhaji Kam Salem - Inspector General of Police,
Chief TA Fagbola - Deputy Inspector General of Police

5. Also with immediate effect, all the present Military Governors, and the Administrator of East Central State, have been relieved of their appointments and retired.

6. As you are already aware, new appointments have been made as follows:

Brigadier TY Danjuma - Chief of Army Staff,
Colonel John Yisa Doko - Chief of Air Staff,

Commodore Michael Adelanwa - Chief of Naval Staff,
Mr. M D Yusuf - Inspector General of Police

New Military Governors have also been appointed for the States as follows:

1. Lt. Col. Muhammed Buhari, North East
2. Colonel George Innih, Midwest
3. Lt. Col. Sani Bello, Kano
4. Captain Adekunle Lawal (Navy), Lagos
5. Lt. Col. Paul Omu, South East
6. Colonel Ibrahim Taiwo, Kwara
7. Captain Akin Aduwo, (Navy), West
8. Col. Anthony Ochefu, East Central
9. Lt. Col. Usman Jibrin, North central
10. Col. Abdullahi Mohammed, Benue-Plateau
11. Lt. Col. Umaru Mohammed, North West
12. Lt. Col. Zamani Lekwot, Rivers

The Structure of Government has been reorganized. There will now be three organs of government at the federal level namely,

(i) The Supreme Military Council
(ii) The National Council of States
(iii) The Federal Executive Council

There will of course continue to be Executive Councils at the State level. The reconstituted Supreme Military Council will comprise the following:

The Head of State and C-in-C of the Armed Forces
Brigadier Olusegun Obasanjo - Chief of Staff, SHQ
Brigadier TY Danjuma - Chief of Army Staff
Commodore Michael Adelanwa - Chief of Naval Staff
Col. John Yisa Doko - Chief of Air Staff
Mr. MD Yusuf - IG of Police
GOCs -

1st Division, Brigadier Julius Akinrinade

2nd Division, Brigadier Martin Adamu
3rd Division, Brigadier Emmanuel Abisoye
L.G.O., Brigadier John Obada

Colonel Joseph Garba
Lt. Col Shehu YarAdua
Brigadier James Oluleye
Brigadier Iliya Bisalla
Colonel Ibrahim Babangida
Lt. Col Muktar Muhammed
Colonel Dan Suleiman
Captain Olufemi Olumide (NN)
Captain H Husaini Abdullahi (NN)
Mr. Adamu Suleman, Commissioner of Police
Lt. Col. Alfred Aduloju
Lt. Commander Godwin Kanu (NN)

All the civil commissioners in the Federal Executive Council are relieved of their appointments with immediate effect. The composition of the new Executive Council will be announced shortly.

Political Program

We will review the political program and make an announcement in due course. In the meantime, a panel will be set up to advice on the question of new states. A panel will also be set up to advice on the question of the federal capital.

With due regard to the 1973 population census, it is now clear that whatever results are announced will not command general acceptance throughout the country. It has, therefore, been decided to cancel the 1973 population census. Accordingly, for planning purposes, the 1963 census figures shall continue to be used.

A panel will be set up to advice on the future of the Interim Common Services Agency (ICSA) and the Eastern States Interim Assets and Liability Agency (ESIALA).

The Second World Black and African Festival of Arts and Culture is postponed in view of the obvious difficulties in providing all the necessary facilities. Consultations will be held with other participating countries with a view to fixing a new date.

Finally, we reaffirm this country's friendship with all countries. Foreign nationals living in Nigeria will be protected. Foreign investments will also be protected. The government will honor all obligations entered into by the previous Governments of the Federation. We will also give continued support to the Organization of African Unity, the United Nations Organization, and the Commonwealth.

Fellow Countrymen, the task ahead of us calls for sacrifice and self discipline at all levels of our society. This government will not tolerate indiscipline. The Government will not condone abuse of office.

I appeal to you all to cooperate with the Government in our endeavor to give this nation a new lease of life. This change of Government has been accomplished without shedding any blood; and we intend to keep it so.

Long live the Federal Republic of Nigeria.

Achievements of the Murtadha Administration

1. Brigadier Muhammed who was later promoted to a General along with some of his compatriots was the first of Nigeria's leaders to instill a sense of timeliness and service. He arrived work everyday on time, just as the lowest ranked employee. But, he tolerated no tardiness whatsoever from anyone including those in executive positions. He led by example.
2. He denied himself the benefit of entourage, sirens and convoys that has become an acceptable way with the

executives, and removed Mercedes Benz (expensive) as the popular official cars for Nigerian executive. His car was not a specially ordered bullet-proof vehicle, neither did he move into the executive mansion.
3. He instilled active and positive service to embolden productivity. In the process he retired, purged, sacked and terminated thousands of employments that were unproductive. He executed it all without any credible charges of favoritism based on religion or ethnicity.
4. His terminations of appointments affected the high and the low because the goal was to move the country forward, avoid waste, and do away with unproductive and corrupt individuals he saw as hindrances to development. He removed corrupt officials promptly. Precise and decisive, he wastes no time after proof he required reaches him, to issue orders to right a wrong. His orders were followed with the words "with immediate effect."
5. Made positive gestures to civilians by filling 12 of the 25 cabinet positions with civilian professionals. He also promised a short military administration long enough to put things back in order for civilians. A promised his Deputy (Chief of Staff) General Olusegun Obasanjo kept by conducting the 1979 elections and ceding to a civilian administration of Alhaji Shehu Shagari.
6. He attempted to ease tension by crossing out the 1973 census figures, challenged by Southern Nigerians in favor of using the 1963 figures. Crossed out all states that ring of regional affiliation. He was a true Nigerian with an objective and progressive outlook on life. His only wife Ajoke was Yoruba, and he had no problem befriending and entrusting people from any region of the country.

Chapter Five

Nigerian Political Challenges

Rotational Presidency Quagmire

Hadiza I. Wada, DBA

December 5, 2009

The issue of rotational presidency has once again surfaced with the current dilemma tabled before Nigerians that their current President may have to soon decide to either resign from his position, or else not run for a second term. Rotational presidency actually contradicts the constitution even if by denying all members of the PDP the same rights to vie for a position the constitution guarantees them, basing that choice on ethnic and regional terms; but also by knitting in saliently some other contradictions. The system allows discrimination against people based on demographics that the Constitution guards against i.e. discrimination based on ethnic, religious and other factors. It also ends up denying all Nigerians their political rights to vie for and be elected President regardless of what part of the country they come from.

Rotational Presidency is a PDP issue and not every party's issue. It was forcefully shoved down the throat of Nigerians by a newly formed party at the most vulnerable yet critical time for Nigerians, i.e. after bringing an end to military rule, and desperately searching for a meaningful way forward. The decision was taken by a few even within the party, and was reached without consultation with the nation as would be expected of any important political decision that has such deep implications for the body polity of the nation. A referendum was never even discussed to see how the nation thinks about it. What is more abhorrent is that it is at variance with the prevailing laws and the dictates of democratic ideals. The fact of the matter is that with such disregard, we now have a cabal of people out to manipulate both law and righteousness for their selfish ends.

Rotational Presidency does not enjoy the backing of the Constitution. The constitution actually extends to every citizen the right to vie for the highest office in the land regardless of where one may have came from in the nation. It is the inalienable right of every citizen. PDP came out in a gangster fashion in my opinion, to announce to the nation before the 1999 elections that it has adopted as part of its party manifesto to rotate between the North and Southern part of the country the office of the President of Nigeria.

Furthermore the South was given the first shot at the seat. President Olusegun Obasanjo was jostled out of Prison in a hurry few months before campaigns, dusted up and practically anointed to run for the office in 1999. The democratic process of allowing all those who want a shot at the seat was muted even within the party. Soon we have an Army General who had ruled Nigeria before, from South Western Nigeria as the presidential candidate for the most popular party. The Western nations, with either good or bad intentions, appear to have waited for the party that has the most chances to win, to usher such a move. Then before you know it, Mr. Obasanjo was made a President.

The Former military Head of State for Nigeria 1976 -1979, Retired General Obasanjo began to enjoy support from Western nations which no Nigerian President has ever enjoyed in Nigeria's history. He dined with every Western President that enjoys the highest powers on the planet, be it in the White House or number 10 Downing Street. The doors were also open to the former President to attend every organizational meeting be it G8, WTO etc whether Nigeria is a member or an observer. Soon everyone cannot mistake the fact that some sort of honeymoon was occurring.

While all this was happening, Nigerians at home were witnessing one of the most tyrannical and bloody regimes in its history. Not only was separation of powers crushed and under constant challenges, there were horrendous incidents of ethnic and religious crisis, one after the other never witnessed at that proportion in previous eras, not even under military regimes. In most of these incidents, the primary targets were either of Northern extraction or else Muslims. It is common knowledge worldwide that Northern Nigeria is majority Muslim, while the South in majority Christians. The crisis unfolded with the first incident being that of attack on Muslim Hausa in Shagamu barely three months into President Obasanjo's regime. It is worth noting however, that the Obasanjo era crises began two years before the United States experience with the twin tower attack that also saw many nations of the world turning against Muslims and their interests globally.

Though Nigerians have not expected a smooth ride during the first democratic government in years after a long period of Military rule, the challenge they faced was of a different kind. They never expected that they will be faced with an ethno religious crisis that will turn a civilian government into one of the bloodiest. This you expect from military rule. The effect of those crises looms large casting shadows that has remained with the nation to this day. The main reason for the continuous tension and enduring insecurity in Nigeria today including reoccurrence of such crisis is because the Nigerian government at that time did not hold the perpetrators accountable for their action, even though the same administration remained in office at least seven more years after the first of such crisis.

Whenever you make laws, no matter how beautifully it seems to address the issues on paper, when you fail to implement them and take them seriously, the public feel they can violate them at will. People take cue from the governing bodies and act accordingly. If you do not have effective law enforcement and serious courts that believe they are accountable to the laws they swore to uphold, and the trust of the people they swore to defend you might as well forget that you have made such laws. Above all these factors is good leadership that is honest and sincere regardless of whose bull is gored. All previous administrations military or civilian have a record of swift control of such crisis, muting it at eruption and punishing culprits whenever appropriate. The Obasanjo regime inherited the same country, people, and their problems as any before it, but made a mark for neglecting timely action and the prosecuting of perpetrators of mass murders.

As serious as issues of taking lives without just cause is, the Obasanjo Administration since 1999 failed to enforce the laws. It failed to show such violators and enemies of security and peace that when they tread on the rights of innocent citizens they govern, they will be made to face the law. Since it was not a new problem, the right time to nip it in the bud was when it first occurred. Failure to prosecute the perpetrators was what gave subsequent violators the strength to continue along the same path; so much so that such crises became prevalent even spilling into the present administration, with reoccurring mass murder incidents in Plateau State.

The same Obasanjo Administration, after failing to perpetuate itself for unlimited terms through constitutional amendment, decided to deceive the same people who I will blame for ceding their rights in the first place. By that I mean Northern Nigerians who have been in the majority since the inception of Nigeria. Not withstanding the fact that had President Obasanjo succeeded in perpetuating himself in power through constitutional amendment, the former President would have willfully and by choice violated the rotational presidency clause of the PDP, cheating the North of its turn for as long as he wished. No one saw the double-crossing nature of that maneuver.

Having failed in the third term agenda, and since the second civilian regime was supposed to go to the North, the former President, based on many media accounts yet to be denied, personally sent for the then Katsina State Governor Umaru Musa 'Yar Adua, who was said to have been asked to vie for Presidency by President Obasanjo. Even at that time Nigerians know very well that President 'Yar Adua was sick.

And here is the twist. Though rotational Presidency does not enjoy the backing of the constitution, the former President knows that the constitution, much like the United State's has enshrined as second in line, the Vice President. So the trick is, should the President be unable to continue, or just run for one term due to his invalid state, another Southerner now by constitutional backing will gain the seat of the President of Nigeria. What a grand design. So today whether anyone likes it or not, just as President Umaru 'Yar Adua has the final word on whether he would resign or else stay on, the Vice President also has a right to demand that he is next in line. The only third option that may deny the two the final say in that matter is when someone legally challenges that provision in a court of law and opens the issue to deliberation and interpretation by the Courts.

The Northern Blunders

Northern Nigeria not by design has found itself almost always supplying the leadership of the country. In a democratic setting where you have a one man one vote rule, the majority will always decide who rules. For all our quarrels and contentions, Nigerians seems to have realized and respected that fact for years. *(See map of Nigeria with what comprised of Northern and Southern States on the next page, 107)* Even during Military times, the military seem to have respected that fact, giving way to the dominance of Northern Military leaders also, except for the forceful entry of General Aguyi Ironsi after a tumultuous episode of the first recorded coup; and also Gen. Olusegun Obasanjo after the assassination of his first in command Former Head of State General Murtadha Muhammad in February 1976.

Northern Nigerians however do not dominate the printed press to date, which until recently has been the most popular advocacy group. They also do not seem to take seriously the need to educate the world in their own words what the realities in Nigeria are from their perspective. The Nigerian Press has been dominated by Southern Nigeria since the (1940s) and after independence from foreign rule in 1960. The Southern press began challenging and painting subjective and inaccurate historic and political picture of the country. On the shoulders of the press more than any other group, in the writer's opinion, lies the burden of strong divisive propaganda that has resulted in a divided nation. They propagate against whatever group they choose. The Nigerian Press being dominated by the South, from inception began an incessant campaign along ethnic and religious lines.

The issues at first were known for what they were regardless of what the papers say. People kept their heads above the water and could decipher the truth for themselves. But for the most part, during the last two decades (twenty plus years), probably beginning from the General Ibrahim Babangida era August 1985 until 1993, the picture became muzzled. The Babangida regime marked the beginning of an era where the corrupt and the hard working civil servant were no different in the eyes of the government. The era of rewarding hard work, accountability; and holding corrupt and inept leaders accountable for their actions ended with the Buhari regime.

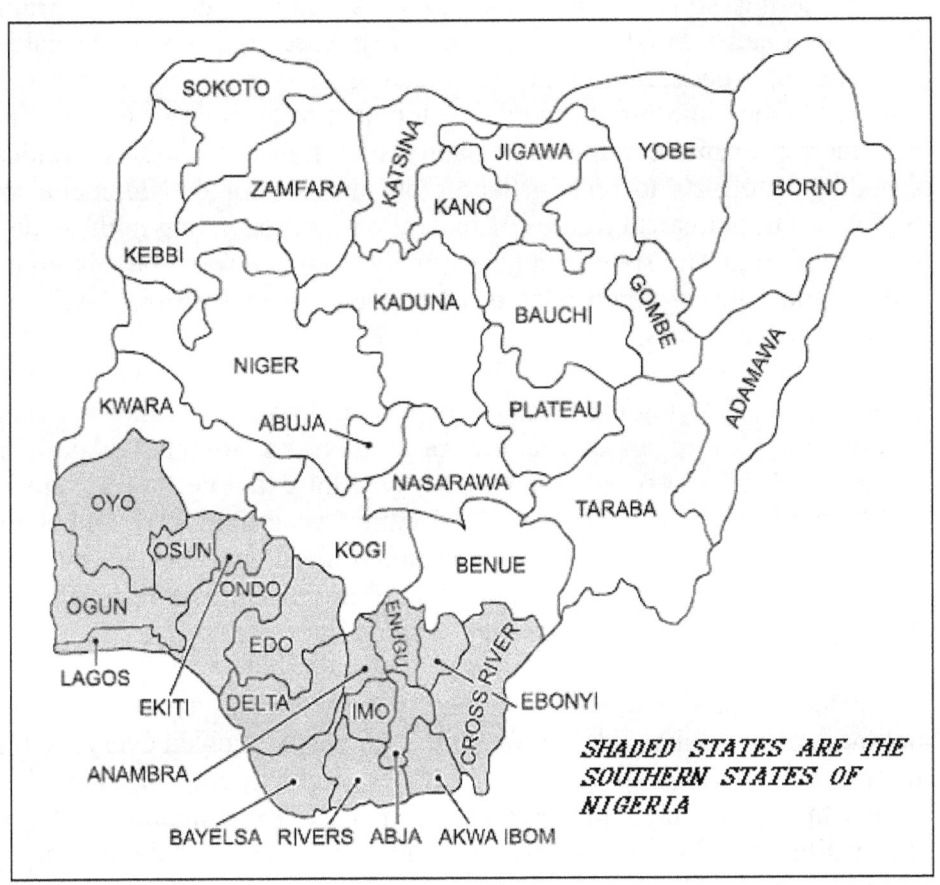

The reporting style of the Nigerian Press since inception, charging Northern Leaders first with ineptitude and later with prejudice paid a lot. The latter generation of northern leaders in trying to prove otherwise pumped money into projects and development to the south. The massive amount for example pumped annually into Lagos, including reckless spending in efforts to reclaim land from the sea for development cost billions. The statistical figures of federal projects spending in those days were alarming. The style paid handsomely, so much so that the Northern part of the country when it comes to developmental projects was to a greater part neglected.

There was no denying the fact that the Gen Babangida regime first came in with an idea of appeasing the minorities and Southern Nigeria in particular. The first set of cabinet positions, for example, saw a majority of positions going to Christians; and ethnic wise the North and South was reflected equally to the proportional detriment of the majority population of the North. Even after the initial cabinet reshuffle, the Babangida regime continued along the same lines.

But what marked the administration the most, and tends to be the hallmark of the Babangida era was the open way it showed everyone that it was not willing to go after corrupt government officials. The "everything goes" mentality was entrenched. It also dismantled many of the institutions that Northern Nigerians were gradually developing in order to coach their people contemporary business skills, such as the Northern Nigerian Development Company NNDC headquartered in Kaduna. The honeymoon with the South did not go beyond the attempt of that administration to build a self made democratic dispensation, with limit to two political parties complete with their ideologies, that all must make a choice as to which to register with as a member.

The result of the Post Babangida era on the nation was blackmail, and hoodwinking of the nation. The press went haywire over the annulment of the 1993 elections, which occurred before the final results were collated and announced. In that election a Southern candidate Moshood Abiola along with his running mate Babagana Kingibe were reportedly favored to win according to the polls. Soon thereafter, the nation witnessed many southern groups such as NADECO and other organizations actively campaigning within and outside Nigeria against the nation. The Southern press raised so much heat, even though that was not the first credible election annulled, neither was it the first time the military has deceived the nation to remain in power or else wriggle it away from civilians by force.

Very soon the Northern majority were willing to lie backwards and allow everyone to set every unconstitutional agenda it wants on the people. The majority succumbed to a very undemocratic maneuver that resulted in an invasion of a cabal of lawless wolves that have today transformed themselves into the realms of party politics in Nigeria. They want to convince the nation that they can now play clean, take care of everyone and play representative politics. They use these dichotomies of North vs. South and Muslim vs. Christian to play games with their electorate, causing irreparable loss of lives and properties. Lawlessness became the vogue and corruption became the norm.

Recommendations and Conclusion

Nigerians have to realize and learn to live with reality. Any rule or administration where the majority is under oppression, and the minorities are forcing themselves on the people through manipulations of various kinds will not augur well for the nation. There is always a limit to oppressing the majority in any nation. That is why even in a country like the United States, a nation that boasts of the most enduring democracy that has lasted beyond two centuries, they have learned to respect the right of the majority at all times. And Nigeria with the North controlling two thirds in land mass, and the two other regions of South West and South East sharing a third of the land mass tells the story to any objective mind.

Despite the fact that population figures do also decide many advantageous gains in the U. S., the United States census is transparent. No one goes out of their way to manipulate the numbers. They even projected after the last census that the White majority will soon become a minority in the 2040s. They work objectively with the numbers they get regardless of how unpalatable it may be to the ruling class which by the way are the white majority today.

Nigerians on the other hand in a very irresponsible manner still rely only on the 1963 census, which the nation and the world do realize is the last most sensible data to gauge the nation's population. The country has attempted many censuses after that but fraud and manipulations have been forcing its rejection. That 1963 census gave the North a majority of population, and in terms of religion Muslims a majority of 47%, Christians 35% and those who claim Traditional religion and atheists 18%.

It is therefore necessary for the nation to be true to itself. Nigeria is not the only country struggling with heterogeneity, but it is one that continues to manipulate itself to destruction. Had the different demographics of the nation come together just like any other heterogeneous nation, then prioritize their developmental objectives based on realities and truth, allocate to people jobs and functions and positions based on merit and expertise and not ethnicity, the nation would have undeniably be the best on the continent of Africa. Both capital and human resources are there to make it a reality.

PDP has dug a deceptive hole for the nation which it labeled rotational presidency. Through it, clear and brazen manipulations are being pulled on the majority. The responsibility principally lies on the shoulders of PDP to lead the nation out of such lawless quagmire. If it does not do that to the satisfaction of the people, the majority should reject it.

As for the overrun opposition that has been crippled by the PDP through both legitimate and mostly illegitimate means, this is the time to rise up and form a righteous and formidable party that gives the nation the genuine mandate of equal opportunity for all: They need to also grow up and quell intra party issues that has weaken them. A conglomerate of different opposition parties can sit and pick the most deserving interests they share and use it to form a party that allows people to run for any office of the land, from the north or south at anytime, in any election session. The nation not only needs such a party, it also needs a strong opposition to check the overzealous one party state Nigeria is turning into.

Let the opposition come together with a formidable party that respects the constitution, and the rule of law. There is no reason whatsoever, that our constitution - following in the footsteps of the US constitution tested and retested for centuries - should choose to go its own way over such an important principle for selfish reasons. Imposing a minority and unpopular government on any nation to appease anyone will never work, because it negates the core value of democracy that gives every person the same right regardless of where he comes from and who he or she is.

I do not by that mean no one from a minority group should run and be elected as President. What I am saying is, it should be open to everyone, and be based on the merits of the person running for office. Anyone from any part of the country can run for any office. If one is judged to be the best to rule by the majority, regardless of where he or she comes from north or south, he should be given the chance. No party should build that unprincipled agenda into itself. And if they do we should reject them.

We should demand right now that that clause be fixed before the next round of elections or we will reject whatever it is the party and its officials try to impose on us. If they refuse to do as we suggest, we come out onto the streets and continue to protest until they respect our genuine interests and demands. Of recent, many nations have peacefully asserted their will that way. In unrelenting peaceful protests on the streets they forced governments that have even celebrated victory to lay down the crown and follow the will of the people. In Ukraine for example, such protests tagged "Orange Revolution" in major cities lasted from November 2004 until January 2005, forcing the government to a fresh re-run of the election, which resulted in the victory for the protesters. We have to rescue the nation and fix it to serve the people and their needs.

Nigeria at a Crossroads

Hadiza Wada, DBA

January 9, 2010

Introduction

Nigeria is at a crossroads presently. It is faced by a man made problem resulting in an anxious leadership situation. The Nigerian President has been reported sick since November, bringing into the fore the need to discuss in an open and sincere fashion how to resolve the issue of rotational presidency the party has adopted. This situation was carefully designed by few self-serving people apparently in conjunction with organizations and interests that do not mean the country well. However, the blame should rest squarely on a few politicians who deceived the nation by introducing a complicated self-serving scheme of Rotational Presidency at the last minute, after the formation of the most promising party to flag off democratic dispensation. Suggesting the system openly at the formative stage may have pushed many potential members away to other parties. So the timing of the announcement must have been planned too.

Politics does not have to be played that way. The lives of millions of people should never be a plot for a play, or a gamble. It should be a serious business that requires extensive planning, and takes up all the energy one has got. This is because even one life is sacred to God and to other humans, not to talk of millions of people and a whole nation. Nations guard lives, property, institutions and even lifeless infrastructures with all their power and resources. They are very serious about that, and they play games only in designated arenas for games.

In Nigeria however, a few people with common vested interest in satisfying their quest for power, control and riches sat and decided the fate of about 140 million people in a way that was not only unjust, but one that no responsible nation will be irresponsible enough to enforce on even a fraction of that population, without a referendum as some sort of approval by majority of the population of Nigeria. One important reason is because it has the potential to cause catastrophic consequences should it fail. It is s selfish system imposed, but unrecognized as a fair system for use anywhere else in the world.

In any sane and normal nation, the basic interests of the people are identified, goals set, laws to support the goals enacted and then how to achieve the goals planned. After all that, then execution of the goals follows. The government leaves no stone unturned thereafter towards achieving the goals for the good of the people. This they do because they believe failure may spell doom for millions of their citizens. Thereafter, any person, organization, company let alone foreign interests all fall below that responsibility to deliver for their people and the nation they are responsible for. Soon the nation is on its way to prosperity.

Any deviation, cheating, undercutting and foul play when the nation starts its journey are quickly identified and eliminated. Nations have gone to war, encountered serious diplomatic wrangling etc when their goals appear to be challenged or derailed by other nations. But in Nigeria, it appears that there are no national goals good enough to dedicate to. Most Nigerians appear to care only about self, hence the abject failure of almost all community institutions. This is augmented by sheer neglect of people's welfare and security for their lives and property, by those in authority.

To demonstrate how neglectful the authorities are about serious national goals; as serious a challenge to basic life and industrial development the issue of sufficient energy (electricity) is, for example, we have seen governments come and go including ones that spent billions of dollars without delivering, and no one cares except some bickering in the legislature which usually die down after the usual commissions eventually get bribed enough.

On the issue of leadership scheming called rotational presidency, the Nigerian media, the people in politics who have led everyone into the quagmire, and our so called intellectuals for one reason or another are not willing to face the issue squarely with an objective mind in an attempt to resolve it. Most are just beating around the bush instead of tabling real solutions that may work. A few people have battered the life of a whole nation by way of gambling on a political table, damning the consequences.

The nation has woken up to one of such consequence and is frozen in time just bickering and yapping at everyone including the President himself, who is also understandably a victim of that grand design. It is crucial to understand that the President may also have been caught in a very difficult situation, where any step he takes has a host of repercussions for the nation, the people, the region he represents based on his party's arrangements, and his political party.

The failure to seriously articulate comprehensive and just solutions is telling. To date no one is coming up with any workable solution that is just, except for the drumming of hand over of power by the region which stands to gain unfairly from the deal while shortchanging another region by clearly breaking the party's own arrangement.

It may as well be because those empowered by the system to resolve the situation participated and still hold stakes in the present game plan. Or they may have come too far, in their plot to come to a realization that the only way forward now is by eschewing their self-serving plots that excludes everyone else but themselves. That the nation is now at a crossroads. The only workable solution appears to be a real solution that not only binds the nation together, but one that works for every single Nigerian. That is the only solution that may today save the nation from becoming a failed state. Anything less may be akin to applying a sticking plaster or masking tape to a raging volcano. It will certainly be a temporary fix that will erupt soon.

Any system that shuts out the majority opinion, vote, voice and people; one that emphasizes our differences not commonality by segmenting leadership to regions of the country in turns, one that denies a universal code of majority rule, and abuses rule by consent of the people is definitely doomed. It is unsupported by law, reason and definitely because of its unjust dispensation, will not expect to enjoy God's blessing.

God is just and works with the truth only, not schemes. The party that got us into this unconstitutional arrangement, the People's Democratic

Party will have to be forced to go back to the drawing table and come out with a just, workable and executable solution that takes into account that Northern Nigeria has not completed its term, should 'Yar Adua choose to resign now, or after just one term of four years. The party has to come up with a solution that allows for the completion of the Northern term.

With both regions having satisfied one eight year leadership each, the Courts, in the interest of Justice should support the universal provision of democratic principles recognized across the globe and dissolve that unconstitutional arrangement. That universal principle of majority rule, as unpalatable to some of Nigeria's anarchists as it is, is the same one the Nigerian constitution adopted. It was forcefully circumvented by PDP.

That principle says every Nigerian citizen from any part of the country has a right to vie for the seat of the presidency at every single election. Nigerians are not the only heterogeneous nation in the world working with that universal principle of majority rule, neither was it the only one patched together by colonial governments. Others in the same shoes such as India, Indonesia, and even others in Africa like Ghana, have gone beyond their differences and colonial past to continue building strong nations.

Another alternative is for a Northerner to step in and complete the first term, should Yar adua resign now. That person a party member of acceptable integrity should arrange a credible and just election next year, without participating in it. At election, the Courts should nullify Rotational Presidency making the next round of election open to every Nigerian from all the political parties, including PDP. The second alternative, though reasonable based on the present dilemma PDP has thrown on the nation, will however shortchange Northern Nigeria by four years, so it is left for them to ascent to it. The courts should also ban any such unconstitutional arrangements across the board for all political parties in the future. This is because it has the propensity to throw the nation into chaos, just as it has done at present.

Other Issues of Neglect

Nigerian Leadership Playing the Ostrich

When people say Nigerians are their worst enemies, you ask what they mean by that. Some recent experience demonstrated that very well. When *The Optimist Voice* organized a conference on Governance and Development in Nigeria on October 31, 2009 we invited a diverse audience and competent speakers to speak on issues of importance to Nigeria. We extended invitations for speaking at the occasion to both Nigerian personalities in government and out of government, and also speakers from among U S professors of Nigerian descent. We did not get a good response from the Nigerian speakers, only those in the U S responded positively.

The event's venue was in the Washington D.C. metro area where not only the U S government has its headquarters that is also where the Nigerian Embassy is located. We invited people from both sides with official stake in what we want to talk about. That was basically a free opportunity for many in the U S to learn about Nigerians and their country.

The conference provided a free opportunity for the Embassy of Nigeria to conduct some public relations and networking, with like minds among policy makers in the U.S. Capital. *The Optimist Voice* solicited not one penny from anyone, including the Nigerian Embassy, to organize the conference. It was a free event for everyone, complete with light food and refreshments, just to make a positive difference for Nigerians, in our own small way.

The Optimist Voice personally delivered invitation packages with copies of relevant information about the conference including speakers, topic and all pertinent information with individual invitations to all members of the U. S. House Subcommittee on Africa and Global Health. We also delivered similar invitations personally to the Acting Ambassador including leaders of various sections of the Nigerian Embassy in Washington D.C.

The irony and most unbelievable response is that, while members of the U. S. House Committee on Africa responded to *The Optimist Voice's* invitation, not one individual from the Nigerian Embassy sees the event as important enough to attend. Not only that, not one person from the Embassy has the courtesy to call and give an excuse for non attendance even if fake, just as a courtesy. To this day it was just total silence.

Though we were certain that attendance from the U. S. House Committee Members that same week will be very difficult giving the vote on Health Care Reform Bill the same week which was forecasted to be very close and uncertain, we just delivered the invitation for reasons of introduction for our publication and for future networking. In reality after some hard thought on our part, we scheduled the event leaning towards making it easier on the speakers and attendees to travel in from various cities. So we chose to schedule it for the weekend.

The response however came only from those same U. S. House Committee Members on Africa who genuinely expressed their regrets for inability to attend given what is ahead of them. I remember receiving a call from one of the Africa Committee members as I was driving to pick up the Award Plaques for our Annual Award winners on Friday, a day before the conference. Honorable Maxine Walters (D-California) asked her personal assistant to make sure she calls to express the Congresswoman's genuine regrets that she would not be able to be present at the conference because she was on her way to her constituency.

The week of the conference, was the same week for voting on Heath Care Reform in the House, as described earlier. And one needs to understand the position of that historical legislation. Health Care Reform is one of the most important reforms the U S legislature and the Obama Administration is undertaking, and it was one of the toughest events the nation had faced in about a century. Yet members of the Africa Committee had time out of their busy schedule to talk to us. The Nigerian Embassy on the other hand chose to neglect us completely.

You are only as strong as your convictions and resolve, so also your motivations and strength of character. In the United States and other serious nations, people take their work seriously. People in elected positions feel an obligation to serve their constituencies and the nation in general, as the law also requires. They try their utmost best to fulfill all those needs. And their impressive response to us, is only commiserate with their obligation to serving within the Committee on Africa, primarily. Compare that with an office such as the Embassy of Nigeria that was basically here to serve the interest of Nigerians and Nigeria as a nation, who chose not to do their job. They are virtually here from thousands of miles to protect Nigerian and all its interests.

What we read from some of the Embassy action was not only that they generally act that way over the years; i.e. they show up usually only when there is some personal and individual benefits to them. In this particular occasion some, we hear, do not want to share the same platform with some of our speakers. In my opinion, this is both cowardly and immature. Instead of representing itself and defending its policies and publicizing itself in the light it wants to be seen, so we can assist in publicizing that live that day, including later online on our site, the representatives of the Nigerian Government (Embassy) would rather not turn up.

As organizers of the conference, *The Optimist Voice* is not siding with any particular opinion nor does it know the details of what every speaker will say. All we did was provide a forum for rich and beneficial discussions. We are however, not downplaying the caliber of the people we invited. Not at all. The voice did its homework to make sure all its speakers and those honored with an award deserved it, backed by credible evidence and documentation. *The Optimist Voice's* aim was to further the goal for which it was formed which includes primarily building Nigeria and its leadership quality and making Nigeria a better nation for its people.

A Hausa Proverb says "You wash your pot, in anticipation of using it the following day to cook." *Don tuwon gobe ake wanke tukunya.* It also says "Preventive steps are way better than cure after illness strikes. *Rigakafi ya fi magani.* These all teach us that one has to keep working proactively towards helping themselves to maintain the positive goals, as well as networking with others, so when something happens they already know who one is. Not only that, through networking with your neighbors early in ordinary times, they get to know you, and can call you to explain to them what you know or think in extraordinary times. You do not isolate yourself, then when something happens, you react.

Our generation grew up in Nigeria with many values taught by our elders. I am talking of those in their late forties and early fifties. Their inherited values have been tested and retested for over a thousand years (of known written history). It was shaped by what they understood from the world around them (culture), as well as the values brought by (religious) emissaries of God. Northern Nigerians in particular have our ancestors bequeathed to us a very rich heritage from those dual sources that it became difficult much later to distinguish between what are devine orders from religion, and what is culture learnt over the centuries. Hence the religious reform that was undertaken in the area of Northern Nigeria in the early 1800's which primarily tackled the issue of separating religion from culture, and resulted in the formation of the Sokoto Caliphate.

Nigerians had such a rich and diverse culture well before Europe decided to take a step further than the exploration of our present day Nigeria by such people as Mungo Park, going further to control the people, their land and resources. Before then for hundreds of years we were part of the "Western Sudan" where great empires, civilizations rose and fell. And these were very rich civilizations, trading across the continent in spices, gold, silver, knowledge, and scholarship. The powerful, even at that time, were able and willing to go on intercontinental travels to fulfill one religious purpose of Pilgrimage, as Mansa Musa did to Makka in the 1300s during the Mali Empire. Mansa Musa was of course a Muslim leader as Malians for centuries were Muslim too.

Today most descendants of those great men are running around in circles exhibiting symptoms of either complete lack of resolve, motivation to help self and others in their communities, or complete ineptitude. Nigerians who appear to be much more endowed to lead the people in the region appear to be one of the worst of them. People cannot walk up to anyone and demand respect if they do not respect themselves. No one accomplishes anything if he is not sincere enough to simply do what he is employed and receive salaries to do. If you cannot fulfill even that, no one respects you or what you have to say period.

Defining the root issue for Budget Implementation

Hadiza Wada, DBA

November 28, 2009

The issue of the budget, and the wrongdoings that we witnessed within the past week, has been with the Nation since its return to democratic form of government a decade ago (in 1999). While holding no brief for anyone, or providing excuses for lapses, the problem of non implementation of budget clearly falls on us all as a people for being too weak to do the right thing most of the time. To find a way to deal with that important deadlock and shackler of development, we need to revisit history. Our aim is to find the problem, isolate it, and device ways of attacking the cancer with the sole aim of eliminating it.

Since the inception of the fourth republic in 1999, when a tough legislator, Speaker Ghali Umar Na'abba insisted that all branches of the institution of governance be allowed to fully exert their roles for a smooth running and take off of the present democratic experimentation, Na'abba, unfortunately for all Nigerians today, did not enjoy as much support as he should have gotten from everyone. The result of that neglect today is, as other structures of democracy continue to mature, that sector of budgetary matters remained in its infancy to date.

Na'abba, a graduate of Political Science knew the importance of what he was talking about, for the good of the nation and its policy. One of Mr. Na'abba's most prominent loggerhead issues with the Presidency (Executive), or the Former Obasanjo Administration at that time was the non implementation of budget, and the autocratic manner in which issues of state that concerns the oversight of the legislature were being mishandled. But Na'abba did not get the support he needed to overcome the hurdle. Not from his colleagues in government, his party, the legislature he was part of, and most especially not from the Press. Some however exert more efforts than others, but the total result was a failure that has today affected each and every individual in many ways.

In August 2002, after three years of unrelenting violations of both the constitutional provisions and the separation of powers, the House gave former President Obasanjo an ultimatum to either resign or face impeachment. After the usual dictatorial tug-of-war, The Speaker of the House, Ghali Na'abba said the House would not withdraw the resolution. Part of the issues in the resolution says past budgetary allocations "were not fully implemented by the executive, despite the fact that all budget projections (monetarily) were met and even surpassed, especially the 2000 and 2001 estimates." This means the spending has gone beyond what was assigned for the projects by the Assembly while what is was supposed to do remain partially done or undone.

As Speaker, Na'abba was the leader of the impeachment movement in the House. By September barely weeks after the impeachment move, the Presidency pulled an anti-graft charge against Na'abba. Na'abba however stayed on course. The House finally seeing how it could open a door to such intimidations against any of them in the future provided immunity to the Speaker. However rumors began to circulate that the Presidency has bribed some members of the House to remove Na'abba from his position as speaker and leader of the House.

Ghali Umar Na'abba was a representative elected from Kano Municipal Constituency to the House in 1999. He was a graduate of Political Science from Ahmadu Bello University Zaria. He contested the election under the banner of the ruling party, PDP. Though a Political Science graduate, he joined politics from a business background being one of few Directors of his family business in Kano municipality named Umaru Na'abba Commercial Trading Company. He soon made his mark as a strong believer in following the dictates of the law, and especially the separation of powers of the three arms of government as enshrined in the Nigerian Constitution, flowing closely in the footsteps of the United States Constitution.

Ghali fought assiduously for separation of powers and most importantly for such dictatorial tendencies that have clouded many important issues coming from the Presidency including budgetary issues, its non implementation, along with actions that hinged on not following the due process of law that clearly violated constitutional provisions along those lines.

Impeachment of the President was tabled for the issue of budget by both the House and Senate without success, though no one, including Nigerian Citizens were in any doubt as to the fact that constitutional provisions were clearly violated and continuingly being violated by the presidency even at that time. The Daily Sun for example writing April 2009 confirmed this by saying "Na'abba at the apogee of his influence was an effective check for an over-bearing Obasanjo. He almost initiated impeachment move against Obasanjo for several impeachable actions."

The Press

The Press who were supposed to be on the lookout for the general public interest holding the government's feet to the fire especially on monetary matters were busy with regional and or clan interest to give the matter the serious attention it deserved. They chased and smeared the Abacha Military Government for no pressing reason but that Abacha had earlier jailed Olusegun Obasanjo. This they did sheepishly, backing the Presidency and Obasanjo Administration, at the expense of such important matters. They also see no problem with the stamping out of Petroleum Trust Fund, PTF, as they did not go after that with any zeal.

PTF at that time had glaringly become the only initiated program from the Abacha Administration that registered significant results so far as public needs were concerned. It was run under the watchful eye of General Muhammadu Buhari at that time and was able to, after many years of military underperformance, reach the grassroots with meaningful development. It began a rapid renewal for growth in areas such as education (school renovations), hospital rehabilitations, provision of duly "PTF" stamped medicine and pharmaceutical products to avoid diversion to private use, road and transport rehabilitation, etc.

For eight years the Obasanjo Administration continued to evade budget implementation, transparency, and accountability for its spending. It effectively bypassed the legislature adamantly refusing to allow it perform its oversight functions at budget implementation inception and follow up. The nation was also left completely in the dark about issues concerning the number one source of income for the budget in the first place, oil resource. The portfolio for Minister of Petroleum Resources remained tucked under the wing of Former President Obasanjo in person for eight years. This has never been done by any administration in the past. Not even under military administration did any Head of State refuse Ministerial Portfolio to anyone assigning it to himself in defiance of law and getting away with it. Not many see any problem with those issues, the press for one did not, and after a while they were completely neglected.

Na'abba was the most prominent fighter, but not the only one. Some Senate Presidents were casualties of the hatchet too. For example, Xinhua News Agency of China reported two years into Obasanjo Presidency that "Nigerian Presidency has vowed to deal with Senate President Anyim Pius Anyim following his allegedly proposed plot to impeach President Olusegun Obasanjo over the non- implementation of federal budgets since 1999, local media reported on Monday." *This Day*, a Nigerian newspaper quoted a presidential aide earlier as saying that "Anyim cannot escape punishment and the top option being considered is his removal as Senate President because the impeachment moves against Obasanjo was his brainchild."

Meanwhile, writing in December 2002 for example Oluwale Arisekola who hails from Ibadan and, therefore, shares ethnicity with President Obasanjo, sees Na'abba as being disrespectful in his utterances towards the President, trying to paint it not for what it was, the truth that yes a problem exists that needs serious attention, but as entho-targeted remark. He further wrote "it is un-African for a 44 year-old person to talk this way to a 64-year old man who could have fathered a person of his age. It showed lack of breeding, proper home training from speaker of house of assembly. Such an uncouth character, I fumed, was a misfit to preside over a chamber of our national legislature."

After a four year fight, Na'abba and many others within and without the party realized that it will be counterproductive not only for the nation but also the Party machinery of PDP to field in Obasanjo for a second term. Na'abba for example, openly campaigned against the reelection of Obasanjo for 2003 Presidential candidate at his constituency of Kano. For that, the Party PDP under directives from the Presidency sealed Na'abba fate with expulsion from the party for "anti party activities." That was not the first attempt from the Presidency to get at Na'abba, but that was the final blow with connivance from PDP at party level.

The National Assembly, NASS for short, started on sound footing at both Chambers from 1999. They raised and rightly so, constitutional provisions that mandates such budgetary oversight. Section 80 of the constitution provides for ensuring that any money spent gets prior approval through an Act of the National Assembly, while Section 88 allows for tracking the money and making sure it was spent accordingly. Chiefly by asserting that provision, NASS leaders took continuous beatings from the Presidency. Leaderships at both house chambers were being changed at the rate of one every year. The House though remained stable after its second leader Na'abba until the end of the first term in 2003.

Reporting on the issue of impeachment over budgetary matters, BBC described the use of the Senate to block the attempt. In one such story from June 19, 2002, BBC reported that:

> *"A behind the scenes deal between Senators has derailed an opposition attempt to force Nigerian President Olusegun Obasanjo to give details of the whereabouts of millions of dollars of public funds. The issue of the funds will now be considered by a senate committee before there is any further discussion in the National Assembly. This is a time-honored practice for blocking discussion of controversial issues by the assembly, according to our Nigeria correspondent, Dan Isaacs.... It is likely to be the death knell for the attempt to embarrass or even impeach the president."*

It should be recalled, as we described earlier, that both houses have earlier suffered various leadership changes clearly visible as attempts by the Presidency to put into position rubber stamp leaders to preside over all actions and policies of the Administration without adequate and proper deliberation. Na'abba was the second speaker since inception of the Obasanjo Administration, while the Senate President Pius Anyim was the third in three years. In fact the removal of Dr. Chuba Okadigbo, the predecessor of Anyim was predicated on allowing Arthur Nzeribe, a senator from Eastern Nigeria, to table a 15 count charge for an impeachment move against the Obasanjo Administration. And just before the impeachment issue Anyim had been under the threat of expulsion from the Presidency over a different matter.

When the House initially issued the ultimatum to the former President Obasanjo on the impeachment he described it as "a joke." But on expiration of the ultimatum for his resignation, the House went ahead and tabled the impeachable offences, 17 of them. Top on the list was "Obasanjo's failure to implement the Appropriation Acts of 1999, 2000, 2001 and 2002, and spending money that was not approved by the National Assembly."

The effort to divide the ranks of the legislators by turning the table against the leadership of the National Assembly was however resisted. Both the Senate President Anyim and the Speaker of the House Na'abba were reported to have quickly removed Obasanjo's sympathizers from their positions in the House and Senate committees.

Obasanjo was reported to have sought the help from his Party PDP and two Former Leaders of the federation Alhaji Shehu Shagari and General Yakubu Gowon to intervene on his behalf, which they did.

The Nation

Most people across the nation appeared to have realized the importance of the issues raised. The issues of budget circumventions and non implementation by the Presidency of Obasanjo and willful spending from the country's coffers without recourse to the power of oversight by the legislature were carried by some press credibly, most especially by the broadcast media which were more effective in publicizing the issues, even if not as in-depth as the printed press. The people the press was serving however did nothing.

Most Western Nigerian press played it down, while other People of Yoruba extraction saw it as an affront to ethnic leadership of a son. Many write ups from the western part of the country the seat of the Yoruba viewed and condemned the move in ethnic terms. Even those from the academia you may think could see the adverse effect of such violations were busy writing articles such as one titled "Why both

Obasanjo and Atiku should not be impeached" written by a regular online columnist from Howard University, Mobolaji Aluko.

"New African" magazine published in London also reported that by October 2002 a group from the Southern part of the country where the president came from waded in on the issue. The group tagged "The Patriots" led by the country's prominent lawyer, the Late Rotimi Williams came up North to Abuja to pacify the legislators, but in the same coin issued a recommendation for the former President not to consider running for a second term. A week after the visit by the William team however, Mr. Obasanjo acquired the necessary papers to formally enter his intention to run for a second term.

The same publication "New African" reported soon thereafter that Obasanjo's response to the ongoing drama was actually two-pronged. While he exploits the good offices of the former heads of state to stop the threat of impeachment, he yet feels bent on vendetta." As such, damaging information continued to be leaked often to put his opponents on the defensive. In October, the press was agog with news of fraud in the defunct Petroleum Trust Fund. The obvious target was Gen Muhammadu Buhari, the PTF former chairman, who is contesting the presidency against Obasanjo on the opposition ANPP ticker."

Conclusions and Recommendations

The scenario above described how everyone failed the nation in their various capacities by dropping the ball on the issue of budgetary implementation in Nigeria for the past decade. No serious nation could even dream of an administration acting that way and being left alone to not only stay in office for its full four year term, but even allowed back for another four years. Without a transparent budget, and other budgetary due process put in place to ensure accountability as well as strict application of funds to carefully sorted and prioritized projects, no nation can succeed in attaining development.

All institutions on whose shoulder rests this important function should rise up and demand that due process be followed in relation to budgetary matters. The legislature should sit up and do their work. The Press should jump on it and demand transparency, accountability and due process, while the people owe it to themselves most especially to say enough is enough. Nigerian citizens should attribute it, and rightly so, as one of the major reasons for the collapse of the country's educational system. No system will survive lack of resources and also accountability for such resources. The matter should not continue to be brushed under the carpet, because of its immense importance in terms of ensuring that whatever is allocated for projects and development has been duly disbursed, tracked and implemented. Peg the money, know the amount allocated and follow its whereabouts (accounting for every penny), up to the conclusion and deliverance of the project.

Chapter Six

Nigerian Security Challenges

Reversing Deterioration

Hadiza Wada, DBA

February 20, 2010

Whenever you bottle up your frustrations and problems trying to convince everyone that they do not exist, you are digging yourself a deeper hole. All your energy is wasted in convincing and persuading others towards your delusional and unreal position. Every psychologist will tell you that the first step towards healing is admitting that you have a problem. Once you do that, the bitter truth comes to the surface, staring you in the face. Your inner self immediately begins working in waking reality and within the subconscious towards finding ways to eliminate the problem, so you may return to normal life of greater ease.

Once you have admitted reality, sincerity in seeking the causes may be acceptable to you. You may also be serious in finding those practices that tend to fuel and feed the problem. By doing that and making laws and policy towards dealing with it, you have set yourself securely on a path to healing. It is for the eradication of problems, management of resources and the establishment of credible infrastructure and systems, that governments were set up in the first place. These are their major functions. No government is worth its name if it does not meet such requirements.

In Nigeria though, time and time again, all those in authority usually do when events and incidents that challenges security occur, is to set up commissions of inquiry hoping that the general public may get off their backs on the assumption that the authorities will do something. And that is exactly where everything stops. No subsequent actions such as policy changes, law making and enforcement are taken. Furthermore, no one is consequently held accountable. In short everything is handled superficially, with no toughness and determination, no matter how serious the situation is. It is something akin to leaving a pack of wolves running loose in areas humans reside, neither chaining them, nor training them to live with humans. You only react when they attack, and even then what you do is give the impression that you are seeking to find out which wolves attacked. The victim gets no attention, while the wolves get away with aggression all the time.

Nigeria in the mid 1970s when my generation was in high school, was as peaceful and secure as any other country, probably even safer than most. I stress giving such examples, to assert to younger generations in their 20s and 30s that Nigeria has not always been in the present state. You can decide at any time of the day or night at that time to set out in your car for any other city without fear of anything happening to you along the way. I had a young uncle fresh out of college, with those employer guarantored car loan financed by the banks. He was naturally hyperactive and would decide on a moment's notice, after a long night of rowdy discussions we use to have with friends and family in Bauchi, to travel to two cities at a stretch.

He might say for example " If I set out at 2:00 AM I will be in Kano by dawn (Fajr). I will spend the whole day taking care of some issues and leave by the evening for Kaduna where I intend to spend the night resting. I Will leave Kaduna the following afternoon by Zuhr and head back home." Mostly he leaves after midnight, but no one gets concerned or stops him, knowing he is usually the most alert person there is. The only concern then from traveling at night is being too exhausted and falling asleep on the wheel. Apart from that, no one expresses concerns or worries whatsoever.

We all remember well how peaceful and serene life was, at least in the part of the country I grew up, the North. Attending an out of state Girls boarding Secondary School, we travel frequently. Privately owned and operated transportation services were everywhere, including state owned regularly and timely run buses. *North East Line* operated by the North Eastern State Government was our regular bus that takes us home after our boarding school closes for vacation, and the private buses were many including one named *Ekene Dili Chukwu*.

Those transportation services for the general public were numerous and travel across the country at anytime, without fear of being stopped or one's passengers being robbed. People and goods move freely and hitch free. Then there were the sixteen wheeler trailers who love to travel all night, when the highways are less congested.

Today, Nigerians choose to follow a different path, where in broad day light you cannot be assured of safe passage from one simple city to another without the fear of being stopped on the highway by armed robbers *('yan kwanta kwanta)*.

The painful part of it all is that, while the problem is pervasive and chronic, our law enforcement is complicit, sometimes even accused as perpetrators of such crimes. At the very least they have been very ineffective at the local as well as federal level. To make matters worse, the state and federal level authorities charged with security for life and property have been so engrossed and preoccupied with trivial issues of less importance to the people, to engage in any serious plan to deal with the endemic security challenge.

Worse still my colleagues in the Nigerian media, instead of identifying and focusing on the issue with a genuine intension to force the authorities to address it, are busy accusing foreign neighbors of being behind Nigeria's security problems. To them Nigerians are such saints that it takes foreigners to perpetrate such untold actions of barricading roads, threatening passengers and private citizens driving along the highways, robbing them of their funds and valuables and ducking back into the wild as poor victims count their losses. And these are daily occurrences on Nigerian roads.

Because no one seriously pointed to or made such issues priority for long, soon such lawless rogues took the issue much further. Today you do not have to leave your home and get onto the highways to begin thinking about your security. Your own law enforcement agents, paid by your government using your state and federal resources to safeguard your lives and properties are the very people that may enter into your homes in broad day light, kill members of your family mercilessly in front of young children, toddlers and babies. Or else seek out young children between the ages of eleven to early twenties take them onto the streets, order them to lie on their faces and shoot them in cold blood.

Well if for long the corrupt governments in cahoots with corrupt and prejudiced security agents, and a look the other way press that blame all security problems on foreigners have managed to deceive themselves and the world, other avenues have surfaced to inform the world about such chronic hypocrisy. With today's portable and hand held technology (such as handsets, pocket sized specialized or digital cameras etc); and a willing international press, such as al Jazeera, willing to do real press work in playing back such captured episode; everything is now in the open. The truth has come to light.

Solution

Nigerians as well as their global well wishers are now sick and tired of the politically correct games that fail to address the issues, played by those in federal leadership positions. They are running out of patience with outright violations of the universal codes of law enforcement by the country's security agents. And they have the least patience for prejudiced and incompetent Governors who swore by their holy books to defend lives and properties of everyone within state borders and under their jurisdictional control, but then turn around and unleash a genocidal wave of crises one after the other on those entrusted to their care.

Those in whose hands lie the power to give the right orders that will set things right at Federal level failed utterly. The reality though is that every elected or appointed position has corresponding authority commiserate with that level. Based on the same kind of rules that are not unique to Nigeria but are universal, other nations of the world consider every security breach serious and face it squarely. That is why they continue on paths of peace. But when a Commander in Chief of a nation allows himself to be gagged by loyalty to his party or other interests than his supreme duty to clamp down on a serious security threat, things will continue to fall apart.

Only in Nigeria, can you shamelessly see gross insubordination by a state level Governor on issues of serious national security. The Commander-in-Chief's first step in 2008 (after the crisis that occured in

November) of sending his army Chief of Staff to assess the situation on the ground in Jos and report back to him was in order. That portrays to any intelligent analyst nationally and abroad that the right steps may follow. But subsequent steps after that was misguided and utterly devoid of any meaningful strategy.

The setting up of a challenging panel under Bola Ajibola, was the greatest embarrassment to the nation, and its kangaroo sitting and the subsequent report were all not worth the paper they were printed on. How can any serious nation in the 21st century begin talking about forcefully taking over people's rightfully owned properties and sending them parking. And these were by far the overwhelming victims of the violence, as witnessed by both national and international sources.

The chair of the state level challenging panel, Bola Ajibola, being a former Attorney General of the Nation is a double negative blow, showing the mindset of Nigerian leaders that appoint such people who display no ethical and moral bearing to resist their own prejudices in favor of their professional integrity. Accepting to serve on such a panel by a professional lawyer who knows fully well the powers conferred to the Commander in Chief of a nation to deal with security threats in any part of the country, tells you a lot about the person, Ajibola.

So now that the problem of security of life and property in Nigeria is undeniably heinous, as carried by all international media; those in whose hand is policy making, law making, including the interpreters of such laws (the courts) will have to step up and do the right thing as expected of them. The deceitful and hypocritical image they paint to the world, faulting every other people, including the victims themselves as the problem has to now be discarded in favor of facing the reality of the problem, and finding real solutions.

The Nigerian people should rise up to the occasion and play visibly corrective roles in shaping their nation's destiny. Tides do turn. If today one thinks because he is up, he does not have to speak and work for the right thing, when the tides turn, as it surely always do, he may be on the receiving end, and may turn out to be playing the legendary "the boy who cried wolf" as no one may offer help.

Addressing Police Inefficiency

Hadiza Wada, DBA

May 22, 2010

In attempting to spotlight the reasons behind police inefficiency which is not particular to Nigeria alone, but many third world countries and African nations in general, we will examine the causes as described by empirical studies. One very useful study was conducted by Alice Hills and published by *The Journal of Modern African Studies* in September of 2007. The study is titled "Police commissioners, presidents and the governance of security."

The study, informed by earlier studies that pinned the major problem to governance of the force, observed and recorded situations from four different countries of Africa, namely Ghana, Zimbabwe, Kenya and Uganda. The findings were similar across the board, with the difference primarily being the extent or intensity of the problem being more pronounced in one country than another.

The police, it was discovered, faced three conflicting roles. (1) There are the donors from abroad (external) who make funds available for improving police work such as the United Kingdom's Department for International Development (DfID) and the Organization for Economic and Cooperative Development (OECD) who promote certain norms and processes on one hand; (2) Internally, there are the civilian authorities, their institutions and their operating practices; the processes they advocate having been developed between governmental departments and civil society; (3) And finally there is the presidency (executive) who usually control the hiring and firing of the highest officer be he Commissioner of Police or Inspector General of Police, depending on country specific title.

Various researches, not just Hill's came to the conclusion that African Police are accountable to just one master, their

Presidents. Police in practice enforce political decisions of their political authorities "and references to democratic forms of accountability are rarely more than tactical consensus or gestures to donors." Hills added that more often than not, police actions in such countries are at variance with the democratic requirements of accountability for their actions. They became political tools at the hands of their prevailing political masters.

Hills studies in fact points out that it is wrong to assess the effectiveness of the police through the mirrors of democratic ideals. Studies that did that, she claims result in inaccurate analysis because the police are in actuality governed by presidential preference. That was why her study tries to figure out the locus of influence within the police by exploring the influence between the police chief and the President. The direct influence observed is remarkable. In Zambia for example, President Mwanawasa was quoted dismissing his Police Chief for doing two things which appear in line with an objective dispensation of his duty, i.e. delaying the arrest of an opposition leader while questioning the legitimacy in legal terms of the President's verbal orders for the arrest.

Hills, and particularly Klantschnig (2009) who specifically studied Nigerian law enforcement in his work titled "The politics of law enforcement in Nigeria" both agree that the governing process is the area that needs to be studied more intensely, with the intention of strengthening and empowering the law enforcement institution, making it more independent of political influence. Klantschnig concludes that his study of Nigeria "confirms views of politicized nature of law enforcement."

The irony of all this is that; while the presidency always target the police for exerting control and using them politically, they know the police are generally powerless, and therefore do not entrust their personal security to them. They usually form a special security unit from intelligence sources, and fill such positions with relatives and close associates they personally trust. Likewise Presidents use special units to deal with special matters, such as the Nigerian Drug Law Enforcement Agency

NDLEA formed to deal with the menace of drug use, trafficking and sale. They do not leave such political pet projects to the inefficient police. In actual fact Hill's study goes on to say "Presidents do not want an effective or efficient police answerable to parliamentary committees or judicial enquiries (some have committed so many crimes that they cannot afford to), but they value the police as a tool for enforcing political decisions, maintaining order, regulating activities and regime representation."

While other security establishments such as the military are empowered, and can generally stand on its own, the police are left to find institutions or organizations to lurch on for resources. For example, in 2005, the Inspector General of Police for Nigeria Mr. Sunday Ehindero was quoted saying "It is disheartening to see policemen live in a kennel...The conditions in some barracks are, to say the least, nauseating." The embarrassing way in which the public help support the police at check points by throwing stipends at them was cited as a means of complementing their meager salaries. It also demeans their status in the public eye.

One would think that with such accounts only uneducated recruits with no options left will aspire to join the police force. But accounts from some educated and seasoned police members will suggest differently. For example, Nuhu Ribadu, the son of the famous Ribadun Yola of cherished memory was a guest of our online publication *The Optimist Voice* last year. He holds both bachelor's and graduate degrees in law, and had worked for the Nigerian Police for about twenty years. He rose through the ranks, and was personally plucked and assigned a new pet project by the former President Olusegun Obasanjo in 2003. Whether the intention was genuine or not, Mr. Ribadu was highly acclaimed as bringing back, even if briefly, the integrity professional integrity of the police force unit, quite rare in African setting.

Hills, however sees the use and manipulations of the police force by Presidents as a tool the former Nigerian President also used. Generally her study described how "Presidents intimidate, constrain and use the police for purposes for which public accountability plays no part." She cited President Obasanjo's frequent hiring and firing of Police chiefs as one such ways. Musliu Smith, the first IG was fired because he displeased the President, while his successor whom to the public was fired because of the scandal of misappropriation of funds after investigations by the EFCC, was actually according to the study probably "sacrificed" to appease donors. Sunday Ehandero however, despite reaching retirement age after coming on board had his tenure extended twice because he was found to be "useful" in carrying out Obasanjo's interests. He bends with the winds in an effort to, regardless of what is right, satisfy the desires of the President.

Klantschnig also appears to back Hills' premise that most studies conducted by donors and the UN do not place any emphasis on the role played by the governance of the police force. He calls such studies superficial using media reports as sources, while the media themselves do not dwell on deeper issues, but street events. For example he says such earlier studies funded externally - though they dwelt much on issue of trafficking and laws in place - did not highlight that heroin and cocaine seizures in Africa account for less than one percent (1%) of global statistics (citing UNDCP 1998: 17-18).

Klantschnig however claims that the pattern of control structure where the head of such projects as NDLEA answers directly to the President helped the project in funding and influence. It set a precedent used later by Presidents for control pattern towards their pet projects. But it is worthwhile to note that the externally funded police force support tend to work for their funding agencies and usually pitching the President's political and personal interest against those of its external sources. And that the experience garnered by presidents, though the hard way, seem to form the basis upon which such presidents form their own pet agencies that came later such as the Economic and Financial Crime Commission EFCC.

Finally in the question and answer section of the conference on good governance organized under the auspices of *The Optimist Voice* last year, Mr. Ribadu, the first police officer to become Chairman for EFCC also pointed out one very critical issue highlighted by Hills studies; i.e. finding ways to strengthen various institutions so they can stand on their own, regardless of who is in political control.

In answering a question on whether there was any need to review and amend the constitution, Ribadu answered that in his opinion (as a legal professional) the Nigerian Constitution is fine. It is adequate as it is to address issues. It is the people who are not willing to work with it, bending the rules the way they like. Politicians and leaders are not willing to act within the bounds of the nation's laws. They act above the law most of the time and that is the problem. It appears to be an African problem, he concluded, where he cited a recent event in Niger, where the President, just one individual, forced the amendment of the constitution after his second tenure was about to expire so he could run for the third time, just as his former Nigerian counterpart Olusegun Obasanjo attempted in 2006, but failed.

The structures that ensure effective governance such as lawmaking (NASS), the courts, the police as institutions, and all other important counterbalancing structures have to be strengthened beyond individual influence of the executive so they could earn the respect and efficiency they deserve for effective service. The nation is yet to achieve that, and any credible effort such as those by House Speaker Ghali Na'abba and some of his counterpart to build the credibility of NASS and its structures in counterbalancing power and checking excesses by the executive was sabotaged by Mr. Obasanjo at the Presidency.

Likewise people such as Ribadu at law enforcement who were effective by far compared to their predecessors, who enjoyed the support of the same Obasanjo for reasons best known to the former President, was kicked out as soon as his employer left office through the influence of those he had made accountable in the past. Mr. Na'abba and Mr. Ribadu along with many others effective at their posts are now out of the loop and forced into exile literally. Even one of the most effective and performing executive, who in spite of the reigning unchecked executive power popular at his time 1999-2007 managed to develop his state, the Bauchi State Governor Ahmed Mu'azu, is among the refugees of hard work; a very discouraging situation.

Niger Delta Issue: Not that Enigmatic

Hadiza Wada, DBA

March 20, 2010

This chapter is a special presentation because no analysis of Nigerian Issues is complete without it. We have not dealt with it comprehensively in our publication, but have just touched on some of its aspects in isolation. It has resurfaced recently however, as one of the most important projects the 'Yar Adua Administration set out to boldly confront, after successive administration have avoided it completely owing to its complexities. To be candid, it was more than a bold move by the administration to make such a decision. Either the Yar Adua Administration was ignorant of the complexities, or else it knowingly decided to take the bull by the horn and might have suffered the consequence. In any case, it is essential to highlight the issues surrounding the Niger Delta crisis to enlighten the general public, as we set out to do generally in this project.

General Introduction

The states that make up the Niger Delta region of Nigeria include Akwa-Ibom, Bayelsa, Cross River, Delta, Edo, and Rivers. These are the states that were carved out of the delta region and its immediate surroundings. The Nigerian delta is where the third longest river of the African continent (Niger) pours out from the West African Coast into the Atlantic Ocean. Some of the major ethnic and linguistic groups that reside in the region long before oil was discovered during the final years of colonial administration in Nigeria were the Ijaw, Ilaje, Itsekiri and Urhobo.

One of the major challenges the communities were undergoing even before the colonial influence was an organizational one. The communities were dissected and living in smaller units as opposed to more complex administrative entities common in other sections of the country. Because of that, the communities were not culturally acclimated with larger and more complex political control, traditional or modern administrative ones. For that reason also when a system of administration was introduced to them, these communities had to learn how to view and consequently adapt them into their cultural leadership dimensions. It was not easy as credibly recorded for years by many objective studies of the phenomena.

One of the bottlenecks identified is that the educated elites among the communities of the Niger Delta, do not exhibit much concern for the population beyond mostly individual self enriching ones. The state governments down to the local governments are very corrupt so that (a) the regular state allocation that gets disbursed to every state of the federation from federal treasury; (b) and the special allocation calculated from the revenue derivation formula that allocates extra percentage amounts to oil producing states; mostly find their way into the pockets of the state government leadership, and especially its corresponding local government councils. A recent study published by the Journal *Africa Today,* (Akinola, 2008) titled "Coping with social Deprivation through Self-Governing Institutions in Oil Communities of Nigeria" concluded thus:

> "Most people in the oil producing region are not benefiting from funds allocated to the local governments – indicating that the problem of corruption and low public morality among the government officials still remain."

The phrase "still remains" from the Akinola paper will suggest to you that it has been a persistent problem. Though inexcusable, one of the problems as enumerated by many sources that study Niger Delta is the lack of strong moral bearing within the cultural background that will for example mandate holding people accountable for violation of public trust in matters of public accountability. Rule of the jungle is more prevalent i.e. survival of the fittest. Akinola calls it "low public morality."

Other writers such as Meagher, K (2006) in her research published by the *Journal of Modern African Studies* describes how it finally took the public themselves to enforce law and order in their own midst to ensure peace, in neighboring Abia, owing to the government's inability to control incessant crime, and broad day light robbery and acquisition by force within the community without recourse to law.

Another problem, which is not frequently brought to the forefront by the Nigerian Press is the fact that those minor ethnic groups feel they have another problem. They feel and complain of the pressure of being marginalized on their own land by a regional ethnic force. The more resourceful regional ethnic group, the Igbo - who neighbor the other minor groups of the Delta - have moved into the inner Delta area in large numbers, many decades ago. The major migration occurred after the discovery of oil. Every Nigerian has a right to move to an area of the country where his skills will be most useful, or get him a better life, so that was not necessarily the problem. The Igbo they felt brought along a problem that has plagued him even in his own states, lawlessness.

Being indisputably one of the most resourceful and commercially enterprising group in Nigeria today, the Ibo seized every opportunity they could see to make money. But they share one major weakness with the ethnic groups of the Delta, and that problem is lack of strong political skills to govern their local communities. The economic interest far outweighs the willingness to play within a set of rules that govern other facets of life of every other Nigerian. But then, these are the laws that make every community peaceful enough to conduct social and economic endeavors in relative peace. Abiding by the law is also what allows one the relative peace needed to enjoy the fruits of one's labor.

The assertion that the Igbo as a group also share the trait of lack of political skills and sacrifice needed by their leadership to build a peaceful and manageable society is all too apparent. It is in fact evident today in Eastern states of the nation occupied by the ethnic group, who have been experiencing leadership upheavals since 1999, when civilian system of government returned to the country. It had been one governorship tussle, re-election, or else court cases over issues of governance.

Meagher gives a more vivid account of efforts by the enterprising Igbo community of Abia State, to provide protection for their shoe trade that was so lucrative that it attracts customers not only internally from other Nigerian states, but regionally from other West and even East African countries like Zaire. After a fierce gunfight between local shoe manufacturing traders and local armed robbery groups, they were able within four months to win over and establish a vigilante group called the "Bakassi Boys."

Akinola in his conclusion also seem to have lost hope in the government's ability to provide the needed security and public trust away from intense corruption. He alludes to that by saying "… self-governing arrangements in the region, where leaders of such groups monitor financial allocations from the government and come together to solve the problems may be able to provide a solution to self deprivation of the Niger Delta or oil producing communities."

Another problem articulated is the invisible hands of the state governments in incidents of attacks, hostage taking and economic sabotage that occur in the Niger Delta region. For years they have been rumored to be used in the price manipulations in the world oil market. Most recently by market speculators that made billions on wall street and other stock markets across the world. By causing trouble and keeping the output from Nigeria low, the nation loses the revenue, while such shortages push up crude prices for stock holders. Oil bunkering is another issue attributed to some of the governors.

Most recently reports of a raid by the Nigerian military uncovered records implicating some state authorities in such criminal activities in the oil region. Leadership, a news publication for example reported that "names of some of the militants' sponsors' minutes of meetings held and account details of the bunkering money paid to prominent chiefs and politicians were recently scrutinized by security chiefs." The incident prompted the Nigerian President Yar Adua to call a special meeting to discuss the issue.

"The meeting held early June, 2009 was reported to be mainly concerned with reviewing the activities of the Joint Task Force (JTF), the militants, the role of the top politicians and the best possible ways of finally resolving the issues that surrounds their differing activities." The meeting occurred well before amnesty was finally hammered. Whether the details of such discussions which reportedly involved all high stake holders in the executive, defense and national security, was instrumental in reaching a way to resolve the issue and signing a deal to end the Delta militancy, only time will tell as situations unfold.

The present administration is not the only one that knew about such involvement of local authorities, but most past administrations military and civilian alike played ball with the issue. In fact the immediate past administration which withheld the oil portfolio was in place when governors such as James Ibori were openly engaged in such games, deceiving the local population with patriotic rhetoric while laundering state treasury, and other illegally acquired funds from bunkering and sabotage, and stashing riches in foreign banks for his personal use. The government did try for the first time to begin to make such governors accountable for their actions, through the use of the EFCC owing to the importance of security in the region. The result was the Ibori and Alamiseigha cases.

The present trend to tackle the Niger Delta issue squarely by recent civilian administrations, especially recent efforts by the Yar'Adua administration, for uplifting the general welfare of its local inhabitants and the nation is commendable. However, only time will tell the effectiveness or true credibility of such efforts. The true position though is, any nation that is endowed with oil has to take seriously issues of security around its oil resources and its corresponding installations. This is not just necessary for guaranteeing internal accountability, it is also necessary because as a competitive stock worldwide, lackadaisical attitude will easily bring in the international commercial vultures. It has been demonstrated in many countries, especially in Africa.

Whenever a precious resource is reported, international vultures start arriving, and the main aim is to destabilize the area and make it ungovernable. Once that happens, while people are busy killing each other, the vultures pounce in and sneak out with the precious resource. This is what has happened and is still happening in Sierra Leone and its diamond mines. It is also happening in Congo because of many solid minerals such as diamonds, copper, tantalite, cobalt etc. Angola was involved in a long crisis and civil war for decades which was generally fronted as a political struggle, while the vultures hide behind the scenes looting. But we have to also remember that Angola is one of Africa's richest in crude oil resources.

If you need present examples involving crude, then you need to look at Sudan whose oil has not long been discovered but its problems have instantly multiplied. They accepted the Chinese to invest in the oil, and suddenly after decades of civil war, it is just recently that the government has been tagged as genocidal, and the country's leader declared wanted by the International Criminal Court, ICC. The war between Iraq and Iran that lasted a few years benefited many developed countries, but when Saddam was not willing to play ball anymore the result is Iraq today.

We have already presented a write-up on corporatocracy and how far they can go with the help of the IMF, World Bank, and their individual governmental policies to get the resources they want, and ensnare the countries they choose. The write-up quoting from many sources including a book titled *Confessions of an Economic Hitman* was published online by *The Optimist Voice* in August 2009. The book, a New York Times bestseller for weeks when it debut in the United States, is not that much of an exposé for many scholars and intellectuals in developing countries who have for years cried out, realizing such tactics being employed against their nations and its interests. It just confirms from an insider, who had worked for such corporations in the past, that such actions were indeed taking place.

One obvious problem though that the government has to address sooner rather than later is the issue of harnessing Nigeria's natural gas. One evident reason to convince Nigerians that most foreign nations are more interested in getting the resource for their own national needs than anything else, is the fact that for all these years, foreign companies operating in the regions (with all the technologies they have and have been using elsewhere for years) have not taken up the issue of harnessing the Nigerian natural gas burned every single day. They dig for the crude and burn up the gas in the process, a clear wastage. The proceeds from the gas would have provided extra billions of dollars a year in revenue for Nigeria, and would have saved the environment from pollution, and the local residents from fighting to live in a polluted environment.

Just Mid last year (2009), Nigeria was reported to have signed a $13 billion gas pipeline deal with Gazprom a Russian Gas Agency, to build a gas pipeline from Nigeria to Europe through the Mediterranean. It was named Tran-Saharan Gas Pipeline Project. The project, though reported as cash strapped, is planned for 2015 completion. The nations involved in the Project ratification because the line will run through those countries include Niger and Algeria. Nigeria in that regard, could use the present anxiety over greenhouse gas and climate change, to make a case for assistance in harnessing its vast gas resources, as against causing pollution by burning it off daily.

Role of Culture

The Nigerian experimentation with various systems of government may look innocent on the face of it. By experimentation the general belief or understanding is that the nation is trying to find a better fit for it. But sometimes it is not the crystallized systems in themselves (presidential or parliamentary) that is to blame for some of the pitfalls the nation continues to fall into time and time again. It appears that many other factors are responsible.

The idea that you can box any diverse group into blanket mannerisms, behaviors, or attitudes is ridiculous, and any objective person should know that. Humans are not inanimate objects like toys that you can simply categorize based on shape, size or color. That is why many people disagree with stereotyping a people or profiling individuals in blankets without taking the time to address them based on their individual character. Humans have individualistic characteristics that make it difficult to easily group them unanimously under any category. Some within a group can be averse to any of the values the community holds collectively, or they can be convinced at any time to move away from a communal value, or even be moved by an internal conviction reached individually to move away from one belief to another.

However community values built over the years can influence a significant majority from a group of people to act in certain ways most of the time. This they do regardless of established laws of the land meant to sanitize the whole nation made up of many other ethnicities; as in Nigeria's case ethnic groups numbering over 200. They continue to risk committing acts that construe violation of national laws because they find it easy to justify the action within their local communities. Such actions that are unlawful on a national level may be an acceptable way of doing things in their cultural setting. In other instances, it is not that the actions are not morally questionable within the community, but the local leadership and elders have neglected the enforcement of such values.

They either lack the moral values themselves, or feel overpowered by prevalence of its violation to do anything about it.

The concept of piling wealth regardless of the means of acquiring it, the countless lives destroyed in the process, and the children wounded from being caught up between the crossfire is a critical topic worthy of discussion. It represents a good example of how crucial issues will be viewed so differently by various groups, making it difficult to have an even handed way of controlling a menace. Corruption, mismanagement and embezzlement; falling educational standard, deaths from adulterated pharmaceutical drugs, falling standards of health care and a host of other menaces could be traced to the problems we set out to discuss in this work. These are some of the menace prevalent in the Niger Delta region, as pointed out by scholars who studied the problems in the region.

The Inception of the Corruption Menace

The menace of corruption becomes more widespread in Nigeria when those sections of the population that were trained to shun it decided they are being left out of the loot. They begin to crave the glitter that came from the lives of those who got rich through the most dubious of ways. In the nineteen seventies to nineteen eighties the Nigerian nation, at least the northern part of the country where the writer lived was generally very peaceful. You can decide at any time of the day or night to travel without ever fearing that someone will block the highway to rob you of anything. News of robberies was something you read in the news coming from other parts of the country, but not the north. The menace of robbery rings, such as one led by a man named Anenie from the southern part of the country at that time was just news to most people. Up North, you can only imagine what it was and meant, but do not have any personal experience to relate to.

Islamic discipline and upbringing that has for long been enshrined into local cultures of northern residents has imposed some basic tenets on the people for a very long time even before the colonization of the country. We recall that Islam was introduced to areas of the country more than a thousand years ago mainly through the Trans Saharan trade across the continent. If you need authentication of this fact you only have to turn to some documented West African incidents from history like Mansa

Musa's trip to perform Hajj more than 700 years ago from the ancient Mali Empire.

Islamic influence and culture was present in West African communities hundreds of years before the colonization of Africa by Europeans. We have to bring to mind always that Sheikh Uthman Bin Fudi (Dan Fodio) was a reformer of an existing religion and its followers, and not a converter. It was after years of use and its degeneration that an Islamic scholar by the name of Sheikh Usman Bin Fudi (b. 1754) began a reformation campaign some two hundred years ago. His campaign swept across most of Northern Nigeria up to and even crossing the Rivers Niger and Benue. The campaign revived the simple principles of Islam.

One cardinal principle of the religion of Islam as practiced in Northern Nigeria at that time stresses the life after death belief, an iconic belief that was bred for thousands of years on the continent, as discussed in chapter one. The revival campaign once again makes it as practical as possible. Funeral rituals of Muslims are very simple, cheap and immediate. The rich and the poor practice the same cost effective principal rituals including the use of simple white clothes, mostly the cheapest in the market to shroud the dead, in humility to God. Some of such basic belief became a hindrance generally in the past, to insane accumulation of wealth that is prevalent today. They also realize the good they do to others and the community in general is what the Eternal God uses to accept them, and in turn care for their progeny even after them. They realize that after one dies, wealth accumulated wrongly becomes useless and may pass to irresponsible children who may squander it, or some relatives if one does not have children. They also realize that accumulated wealth may only benefit the accumulator while he is alive.

Among some of our Southern brethren however, their traditional beliefs generally reigns to this day overshadowing whatever of the Scriptural faith they acquired later. It is true to this day that there exists among various ethnicities within the nation, those who believe that when you die you can take with you all your wealth to the next world. Other burial rights further exacerbate the problem. That belief and practice makes a huge difference in the mental make up of its adherents.

Whenever our cultural values cherishes and supports an act, it makes it easier for people to engage in it. Some cultures believe in materialism with a very loose moral order guiding or restricting how one gets and keep material wealth. The culture supports the position that one can keep accumulating wealth and retain it forever even beyond death. This writer recollects in the late seventies during the Shagari Administration when the father of one of the reigning state governors named Ambrose Ali died, the press had various stories about the riches that the deceased was taking with him to the grave. It was so much publicized - which appears to be one of the main aims of this type of ritual, i.e. letting people know how much riches was spent in the funeral. The attention it drew enticed robbers. Immediately after the funeral, it was reported that thieves paid the grave a visit and looted all that was buried with the deceased. The state governor was very furious and called the act a defilement of his father's grave. So we have such cultures that seem to promote that whatever you covet, you can keep forever. The percentage of such communities in Nigeria, is what the writer may not be able to give you any accurate figure on at this moment.

The deeper truth however is that even those communities that have some part of their culture supporting excessive accumulation of wealth, if you check, you may find that in the past their people do mind how they get their wealth. Just last week, this writer came across an interesting article about corruption written by someone who shares the same cultural background with a corrupt state governor in Nigeria. He was expressing his disgust that his community's values were being mocked at by a greater number of people nowadays. And he cited the past where he says such actions do not occur as often, and even if they do people ostracize the corrupt official so much so that others feel it is not worth their time to go the same way. But today, he added, the same corrupt governor is being invited by local chiefs and other organizations to be a patron, guest speaker etc at their fund raising events.

Commenting on the online article about how shamelessly people engage in such acts, someone else wrote that "shame has boarded a boat since the 1980s and has left Nigeria." It was funny but true. Today no community in the nation is exempt from deterioration of moral and ethical values, North, East, South and West. The leadership, whom people naturally look up to for guidance, are the ones leading the nation in such blind pursuit of wealth accumulation indiscriminately. They break the laws without second thought, and then expect their subjects to be law abiding. They bankrupt their own people, and then sneak it out in secret to banks in other nations. And because they do not want to get caught, they choose banks such as the ones in Switzerland that have policies of secrecy, and as a result when they die not only has the nation lost that money, their kith and kin may never be able to get the money, that is if they even know the bank account exist.

As for the Muslims who engage in such practices, I will call on them to recollect what will happen to each individual in the hereafter during trials, when they stand before their Lord. An authentic hadith describes the Prophet of Islam asking his companions whether they know who the bankrupt person is. They, as expected replied, someone who has lost all his riches and is penniless. Wrong was the Prophet's reply. The bankrupt according to the hadith is a Muslim believer who on the day of judgment comes in with a full account of (good works) Salat (Prayers), Fasting, Zakat (almsgiving and charity) etc but when others he had wronged while he was alive on earth ask for their compensation for his exigencies against them, all his works are reduced gradually paying back those people until he has nothing left to save himself with. After that, if more people come to be accorded justice and he has no more good works to pay them, then their sins are removed from their scales in accordance to the weight of his violation of their rights and heaped on his scale of wrong doing until he piles a lot of bad works from those he wronged; and with no good works left, he gets condemned.

Now if we take a look at ministers, governors, and even simple administrators of hospitals who stole funds from the people's treasury thereby making hundreds of thousands to millions of people go sick, hungry, and lacking quality education to improve their lives etc; one wonders how much work one individual can perform in his lifetime that will erase the bad deeds he earns from wronging such a large population. Even if, lets say, he wronged just a hundred thousand souls (100,000). This is one fact everyone needs to remember when he is in the process of conniving to steal from resources meant for taking care of people (public service) one has sworn by his holy book to take care of. Even if he has not practically taken an oath to serve his people, any government position is created based on some need to serve people. Violation of that trust to serve objectively and righteously opens one to prosecution either in this world, or the next, or both. So the position one occupies means just that, i.e. he executes the duties of the position to the best of his abilities for the smooth running of people's affairs. If served well, such a position will be a blessing with every good work to the multitudes, but if not it leads to perdition.

How we got there

There are several stages of corruption that the nation went through in its life history and it is critical we identify that in order to find ways of arresting the situation. During the colonial administration, natives were engaged in sabotage and embezzlement from the coffers of colonial government deeming it a nationalistic duty of getting back what might otherwise be shipped out of the country to Europe. The act does not stop at taking away resources and funds, but it also involved destruction of properties, buildings and other structures all seen as part of nationalistic agitation for self-government. It was deemed as stealing from a thief who was looting away from the nation to his country in Europe.

But beginning from the initiation of self-government as explained by many writers, people continued to view government funds and property not as national resources owned by the nation for improving the lives of its people, but continued to view it as something outside of themselves that they can loot. When demonstrating or showing their frustration with policies, decisions and other issues, people will burn down buildings, schools, cars, buses etc, which actually is akin to destroying their own properties for it all comes from their own share of the national cake. And the mindset that people carry along with them that government property does not belong to them is more of a chronic problem up north than anywhere. The first stage or category of corruption has not yet left us to date.

The second stage does not appear to have a basis. A writer Jibrin Ibrahim (Ibrahim, 2003) is of the opinion that corruption in public service has been there for many years, since the inception of self government, and he provided the proof for that. Ibrahim described public corruption to have reared its head early during the first civilian regime and even before independence. "In 1957, The Forster Sutton

Commission found that Nnamdi Azikwe had placed public funds in his private bank, the African Continental Bank. In 1963, it was the turn of the Coker Commission to reveal that, in the Western Region, (Obafemi) Awolowo had appropriated public resources for his own personal use." The Northern counterpart independence activist, though escaping such early traces of corruption, joined the band wagon later during military rule. Although it did not initiate it, according to Ibrahim, the Nigerian military entrenched the culture of corruption and misappropriation, says Ibrahim. "Under the administrations of (Ibrahim) Babangida, (Sani) Abacha and (Abdulsalami) Abubakar, what used to be known as corruption became the art of government itself (pg. 27). Until today, The Presidency, Ministry of Finance and Central Bank all have to be paid a percentage before the release of statutory allocations for running the various departments of the government."

Recommendations and Solutions

I believe the reader is interested in solutions otherwise he or she might not have read thus far into the book. People generally want to do something about the situation, if only they could understand why it is happening, from where is it emanating, and how do they go about dealing with it. A typical example of how this was demonstrated was when our publication *The Optimist Voice* held a conference in the city of College Park, the outskirts of Washington D.C. on good governance and development last year 2009.

It was a very emotionally charged gathering at the conference. Concerned Nigerians from different professional backgrounds met to listen to and discuss various challenges that Nigeria faces presently, a decade after the return of civilian administration.

The Guest speaker at the occasion was Professor Buba Misawa of Washington Jefferson University, Pennsylvania. As his voice rings across the room, his deep knowledge of politics, and his experience teaching it for years at a college in the world's most enduring democracy (the United States), plus his knowledge of Nigeria's experimentation with democracy as a system brought a unique mix rarely combined in one individual.

Everyone was eager to find the solution to Nigerian problems of governance. The room was quite, and the faces though in thought and reflection, were also fixed at the speaker. You can hear a pin drop. Everyone knows that there are challenges and problems, but it takes someone with the professionalism in that arena to unwind the puzzle and set the records straight.

By the time the presentation was over, most faces were not only reflecting, but you could feel that they, at the very least, feel that something has to be done to set things straight. A nation with such vast potentials as Nigeria cannot afford to continue to be adrift across the sea of hopelessness.

At the hallway, after the event, small groups of people were still discussing what they feel and believe in. Others such as a group of youths were also engrossed in discussions. Earlier during the presentation, one of them eagerly got up to ask the speaker to please support them and give them direction. "We are confident we can do something, and we are willing. Just what would you advice that we do?" That statement followed an answer from Mr. Misawa, to another individual who wanted to learn some advice on what needs to be done, and how they as youths can chip in to do it.

Organizing interest groups and NGOs with specified goals and pushing for action as a group is one effective way of forcing the government onto any path that leads to performance. That is true in any nation across the world, was the answer. Power by its nature does not answer to anyone's desires and demands, unless it is pushed onto a path strongly and by force from the people who empowered it in the first place. That is an area Nigerians have not yet developed. By not pushing in the opposite direction, they become complicit in oppressing themselves.

Another face hard to forget, was that of another individual who walking away said; "I feel empowered, but I feel angered at the same time." And he surely looked it. "These so called leaders back home fail to know that they have forced all of us into exile, by forcing us into a decision to stay in a foreign land struggling through thick and thin, just to secure the future of our children and their education."

As the nation is close to another round of electioneering, political campaign and candidacy, this is the time for serious discussions. No true Nigerian should sit back and allow others to decide their fate the way they want. Everyone must be on board to ensure that people held up as the candidates to represent them are good and caring enough to deliver on their prioritized needs. This is a time to organize in your neighborhood, keep your ears open for who they are thinking of fielding to represent you. And it is also the time to ensure that the election process and its institution INEC is sound enough to return the real winner, free of subjective influence and rigging.

Another great speaker who took questions from eager Nigerians was the former Chairman of the Economic and Financial Crimes Commission EFCC, Malam Nuhu Ribadu. He was an award recipient at the occasion. Ribadu is a graduate of law from Ahmadu Bello University Zaria, where he obtained both Bachelors and Masters Degrees. He also attended and passed the mandatory one year Nigerian law school in 1984. Mr. Ribadu has revived the hope of many Nigerians wherever they are, that the fight against corruption in high places is achievable.

Mr. Ribadu's career began within the Police Force, but came into prominence in Nigeria after his appointment as Nigeria's Anti-Corruption Czar. Ribadu has been highly proclaimed as a pioneer in anti corruption; having been appointed Chairman to Economic and Financial Crimes Commission EFCC in 2003, after a like agency ICPC has been in place much earlier and been pretty much ineffective. In no time, and within the span of four years, until practically the end of his employer's administration, he had brought charges against both current and former government public appointees including Ministers, Bank Officials, past as well as serving State Governors etc.

That was a great achievement in Nigerian terms, where for years, practically since the early eighties, public accountability has eluded the nation. Nothing like it has been seen before. And even by international standards, one rarely finds a subordinate charging his boss, but it happened when Mr. Ribadu brought charges against the Inspector General of Police where after initial wrangling, his boss (Tafa Balogun) returned to the nation's coffers some 150 million Pounds Sterling under a plea bargain.

Among the politicians as we all know, are some of the most corrupt individuals. To do justice to politicians whom we mostly blame, but who have a few torch bearers among them, we also honored at that conference a former state governor who in our opinion also serves as a good example of good governance for the upcoming generation. We honored Alhaji Ahmadu Adamu Mu'azu former civilian governor of Bauchi State because his performance was outstanding compared to most of his contemporaries. These were the first set of governors who were in positions of power in 1999 after some fifteen years of military administration.

His Excellency Ahmadu Adamu Mu'azu was elected Civilian Governor of Bauchi State under the banner of the ruling People's Democratic Party in 1999. He holds one Bachelor and two Masters Degrees in Quantity Surveying, Construction Management and Construction Economics. Before vying for the seat of governorship, he was one of the regions seasoned business men, in the private sector.

Governor Mu'azu was the thirteenth individual to administer Bauchi State and the third democratically elected State Governor. The twenty three year old state at his inception, (created in 1976), has seen a string of 12 civilian and military administrators but not the like of Governor Mu'azu. For a nation of 36 states, to repeatedly come up among the top three performers during the final year of that administration is an honor, and has vindicated our choice. For Bauchi at least he was a God send.

Governor Mu'azu is arguably the best Governor Bauchi has ever seen. He worked hard in many areas including road constructions within and outside the capital; construction of one of the most modern and well equipped city libraries complete with computers. His housing program and especially his liberal commercial policy attracted many businesses into the state.

It was not only the visible performance one sees everywhere; one thing that sets him apart from his contemporaries is his pioneering initiatives. He conceives and executes programs never envisaged before. And to date many states neighboring as well as far are emulating his initiatives in their own domains. His style of personally visiting without fanfare various projects and constructions, calling contractors to order saved the state much needed resources and white elephant projects common across the country.

Probably one of his most outstanding achievements is investing in the state's most lucrative cash cow, its tourist attraction Yankari National Park, where almost a year before his eight years tenure ended, he freed it from federal control having developed it well with paved roads leading to it, international standard hotels around it, and transportation. Urban and rural electrification is another achievement and is very visible, as all villages leading to and from major cities could boast of light having been connected to the national grid. These are just some of Governor Mu'azu achievements.

We tried that day in our small way to raise Ribadu and Mu'azu as torch bearers for the nation and the upcoming generation. To tell everyone that it is possible, and though people like Ribadu and Mu'azu are rare, they are here and others can be like them if they try. By that, we hope to keep that torch shining; and hope alive.

Chapter Seven

Recognizing Leadership Potential

Hadiza Wada (DBA)

August 29, 2009

As Nigerians move along towards 2011, less than two years to elections, everyone should give ample time to discussing how to elect effective leaders. Leadership makes a great difference in the life of a nation and its people. It is a subject matter that has captured the attention of many intellectuals for centuries. The art of nomination and candidacy is something that should ordinarily be the arena of the governed and the concern of everyone, as it starts the process of representation from local, state, up to federal levels. In Nigeria, it is especially important that people learn and apply better techniques of influencing the process so they could continue to improve the clique of leaders that emerge to run the country. To identify better leaders we have to go as far back as defining leadership itself, then see who it is that fit that definition better.

Scholars of management and administration will tell you that leadership is a process and not a position. The premise is; leadership can only exist with the availability of followers. Among the many definitions of leadership that manifests this premise, is "The process of influencing an organized group towards accomplishing goals" (Roach and Behling, 1984). By such definition, one understands that the difference between chaos – defined as a situation of breakdown of law and order – and a smooth running operation is organization and leadership. But equally important are the followers without whom the question of leadership will not even arise. A third and final arm is situation i.e. some common interest or need that makes the people (followers) feel they need a leader. Leadership in the social sciences therefore, is understood to be a process involving three arms or segments; a leader, followers and situation. To illustrate the three definitional segments, let us look at just one leadership style:

Inspirational Leadership

Inspirational leaders often emerge when a society is in some dire situation or a state of hopelessness. They then inspire the community through their gift of eloquence of speech and power of words. Some of such leaders include Martin Luther King, Malcolm X and a host of others who emerged during the civil rights movement in the United States to lead their communities to greater freedom. They inspired their communities to rise up, so they could lead them out of their existing situation. In applying the premise of leadership definition, the situation (racial oppression and discrimination) existed well before Reverend King (Christian) and Minister X (Muslim) were born. The followers, mainly the black and African American communities nationwide, were also present well before the two began their movement or organization against the established system that they found oppressive. But these inspirational leaders possessed the ability to stir the emotional side of their people to such a level that their followers felt empowered with an attitude and the zeal for demanding a way out of their oppressive situation.

Inspirational leaders do not usually aspire to hold political offices, and may not necessarily make good political leaders because their background is religious and not political. But they do contribute significantly in stirring a great multitude of the people to be active participants in shaping their destiny. They force the ruling class or party to listen and measure up. What contributed significantly to the success of Malcolm and Martin for example was their religious backgrounds that provided some moral, ethical and spiritual bearing. Because their message was backed by the manifest truth of religion, the politicians knew better than to confront and challenge them directly. They had to find alternative and covert ways of silencing them, and both suffered the same fate ultimately.

But politicians need some degree of inspirational leadership also, to be able to attract and keep some followers. In the words of Ted Turner the founder of CNN:

"It is hard to be a leader unless you have some kind of passion for something ... Inspiration and passion usually go together. If you are going to try to persuade others to go with you, it certainly doesn't hurt that you've got very strong conviction about where you are going. Like Columbus did, for instance, to discover the new world. And, if you got passion and conviction, you are more likely to be inspired. If you are inspired yourself and passionate about something, you are more likely to succeed at it, and you are more likely to get others to come with you."

The Various Aspects of Leadership Potential

So while some believe that leaders are born with a propensity for leadership, and some are gifted to inspire the people and lead, to the scholars of management and administration that is only a fraction of the truth, for they consider leadership both an art and a science. They stress that while scholarship may not be a prerequisite for leadership effectiveness, understanding some of the major research findings can help leadership better analyze situations, using a variety of perspectives available to them. In short scholars of management and administration believe both knowledge (learned) and the practical exercise of leadership in the past (experience) and also leadership qualities (personality profile and leadership traits) contribute to a greater extent to leadership success.

It appears from the above description of leadership that Nigerians seem to prefer assessing just the personality. "I think he is a good person, so I will consent to his candidacy." That alone is not enough a screening for someone that will impact your life and that of your children, and even your aging parents and extended family for the upcoming four to eight years. It is essential that communities and voters assess a candidate's background as to knowledge (education), and experience in either government or private practice; making inferences as to what applicable experience he might have acquired from such a job or profession. Finally – and that does not mean the least important of all - they assess his personal character.

A person being likable or "good" does not automatically mean that he or she has what it takes to check plunder and abuse of office, a major cause of concern in Nigerian governance. That requires additional conviction and the guts to establish and maintain the necessary checks in place to arrest embezzlement and prosecute those who managed to outsmart the rules for their personal gains. Being good and of good nature does not also mean the person could run a government including tracking and making wise use of your state or federal resources. Relevant track record from past services is essential and extremely important. If those qualities are also present, then good character is adequately backed by conviction and action. "Leaders do the right thing. They choose character. Leaders avoid shortcuts where ethics are abbreviated. They calibrate the consequences of their actions and send that clear message to their associates. ... Leaders set the example. They cultivate commitment and inspire admiration and respect for the institutional values...," (Danzig, 1998).

Another person who is also recognized as one of those who have exhibited and earned respect in the field of leadership says "it is a matter of great concern to me that the modern slogan for the pursuit of happiness and success has become "knowledge is power." It is my hope for planet earth that the leaders of the twenty first century adopt the slogan "Integrity is power." We dare not the explosive development of science and technology obliterate the development of character as the driving force for man's behavior." - General Robert McDermott, USA.

Leadership qualities go a long way in defining a person in position of leadership. Such qualities include, being innovative, inspirational, or possessing vision and foresight. Leaders are prone to taking on new unforeseen challenges without hesitation and applying various strategies to effectively overcome them. Not to be confused with management, leadership is found to be more flexible, innovative and open to changes and challenges, while managers are more identified with qualities such as controlling, strict application of explicit and tacit organizational norms and rules, maintenance of status quo and the like. Managers in short run a unit in compliance with orders and expectations from their executives.

In fact in Nigerian situation, I have observed more managerial traits than those of leadership in many highly placed political office holders who have been elected into positions of leadership, and that should not be the case. A leader with no vision and innovative ideas and solutions to the unique challenges in his domain generally turns out to be oppressive, for he "manages" situations as they arise in order to please others, with no deep understanding of his task. He does not seek to find, neither does he create an avenue to solicit for problems from his voters into office. He does not allow his staff and associates to objectively brainstorm with him and guide him to those needs. In fact sometimes it is his subordinates that shield him from his constituents. No long-term and innovative ideas and solutions are pursued. To compound matters, such a leader forces his immediate staff to be zombies, following his whims, with no justifiable rationale. That is one of the main reasons why today most elected leaders in Nigeria cannot ascend the podium and proudly describe their achievements.

Many a best seller book offer valuable advice on leadership and leadership qualities. Some even crystallize some characteristics or habits of successful leaders for those interested in emulating them (e.g. The Leadership Traits of the Geeks and Geezers). While they are also valuable in the quest for defining and recognizing those people who may be better leaders in any given situation, to the scholars of management, such books offer maxims (Hughes, Ginnett & Curphy, 2002). Maxims are someone's personal opinion that offers valuable advice about a subject matter. The scientific alternative to leadership maxims is leadership theory.

A leadership theory is based on tested and retested ideas about leadership that have consistently come true so as to be accepted as applicable facts. In the science of leadership, some process is mandated to make sure that the result of the study is acceptable as scientific fact. Though both leadership maxims and leadership theories are useful for the understanding of the complexities of leadership, in general only theories contribute to a body of knowledge concerning the science of leadership. In short just buying and reading some of those books about leadership habits and traits do not cut it. While useful, do not put all your bet on a book, you should know there are other alternatives that provide better proven leadership aspects out there.

Power

What about power? Scholars define power as "the capacity to produce effects on others" (House, 1984); or else the potential to influence others (Bass, 1990). Legitimate leadership has to be empowered through some process. Whereas power is the capacity to cause change, influence is defined by scholars as the degree of actual change in a target person's attitudes, values, beliefs and behaviors. In our quest for defining leadership, its potential and finding who should lead, how do we identify the ones who possess the right qualities? In doing so it is essential to find out the basis of that power. In short before we choose a leader, we need to dig into his or her background to find the basis, and decide for ourselves whether the basis of that power provides the individual enough backing and resources for being productive in the position he is aspiring to occupy. Apart from being certified productive we may also want to find out if the person is willing to do the job the right way as expected, based on personality. These are two different things. For example, being the most gifted banker intellectually does not qualify a renowned thief to hold a position of trust in a bank. Let us look again at some of those foundations of power.

Scholars of management and administration (Ravens, 1959) classified the basis of power into five (5); Expert power, Referent power, Legitimate power, Reward power and Coercive power. Expert power is backed by knowledge. A surgeon may for example exert considerable influence in a hospital because other employees and professionals depend on his knowledge, skill and also judgment, though in reality he or she may not have any formal authority over them, in short they may not be answerable to him administratively.

Expert power is a function of the amount and quality of knowledge one person possesses relative to the rest of the group members. In fact he is the expert among the group, and as such others have to follow his lead and orders in order to do their job well. Referent power refers to the raw potential influence one has over the rest of the group, in a given situation. Other group members have acknowledged this position in some way, which may have grown over time.

Legitimate power on the other hand is formal and officially conferred on one through some laid down process. It is more applicable in politics where you gain that power through election to the position. Reward power however, is the potential to influence others due to ones control over some desired resources, for example the power to give raises, bonuses, positions, appointments and promotions. Coercive power is self explanatory. One who wields coercive power influences the followers' action through fear of punishment, or loss of valued resource. So also the power to deny employment positions, appointment or promotion.

Conclusion

In light of the above, it will greatly benefit each community to stand up and make sure that their candidates for offices at the local, state and federal level are all people of repute with ample qualifications for the offices. And that they have what it takes based on all the above identified criteria; personality-wise, track record wise (background experience), educational and knowledge wise, and that they have both the moral aptitude plus the strength and courage needed to check unnecessary embezzlement and waste. Finally the electorate should demand that they have already exhibited the trustworthiness aspect in some previous positions i.e. the consciousness and moral aptitude to feel that they are humble servants of all the people that have elected them. And that they have the capacity to hold that trust, knowing that the electorate look up to them to safeguard and protect their lives and property, and also make better their lives and that of their children.

Frankly, the situation is not as hopeless as people might think. If every community at the local government level where their families reside and their influence is greater decide to organize to ensure that only the reputable, able and qualified contest one against the other; then whoever emerge should be the best among them and therefore the most qualified to represent them. With such changes at grassroots level, those who eventually make it to the federal level will represent them well and make sure their voices are heard. And people at the helm of governance at Abuja will be forced to listen. This is not a choice, but a requirement, to rise up to the challenge and better the lot of your people and community. With the abysmal level situations have reached, no one expects changes to happen by themselves without a vibrant followership or electorate that are proactive to the situations that have plagued them. It has to start from those who feel the pain of leadership the most. For those of us who are Muslims, we do know that Almighty Allah Himself says in Suratul Ra'd (Quran 13:11) "Verily never will Allah change the condition of a people until they change what is within themselves."

Chapter Eight

Nigerian Educational Challenges

African Educational Challenges

"History shows that it does not matter who is in power...those who have not learned to do for themselves and have to depend solely on others never obtain any more rights or privileges in the end, than they had in the beginning" **(Dr. Carter Goodwin Woodson).**

The quote comes from an educator who became a household name in his era because of his opinion about the effect of education or lack thereof on African American community of the United States. Such discourse is very important in coming to grips with the failures of the Nigerian and other African educational institutions. It lays bare the possible causes of ineffectiveness or non performance by graduating students of modern education worldwide.

Carter G Woodson, writing in the 1930s opines that the primary culprit is the effect of contemporary educational curricula and teaching processes on non white people of the world in general and black people in particular. Mr. Woodson is a well known African American who had served as an educator for about forty years in different regions of the United States. He came to the conclusion that contemporary curricula that berates and despises African contribution to the world goes out of its way to shortchange the colored person.

Such an education when attained by Africans tends to mis-educate them, opines Woodson. The most educated of them leave colleges with knowledge that could hardly be applied to help their people, because they read and were made to adore Shakespeare, Aristotle and Plato, Latin and Greek Philosophy a completely different ideology and way of thinking than theirs. And to make matters worse, they were taught to hate and despise themselves, crushing any motivation they may have had to even try.

Though the opinion was based on the educational problems encountered by the African Americans in the United States, if you look at the premise used and the general ideas, they apply worldwide. In fact the writer mentioned also African states which were at that time still under colonial governments, as undergoing similar experiences. And not many countries to date have completely revolutionized their educational systems, revising and rewriting their textbooks to teach their children what they need to understand and from what perspective. It is therefore not much different even today.

The idea that the best philosophy, literature, analysis on life, all systems of life like how houses are built, how hospitals are run, how schools should teach and what they should teach; if you let someone with no interest in your welfare design it for you, you may never live to your full potential. The best you can be is yourself, for you can never be someone else, you can only try your best. As the vendetta to keep slavery alive waned, and the civil war fought to maintain it failed to give victory to those who advocate continued slavery, the colored minorities began to push for changes including in areas of education. They still are doing that for the playing field is still not equal.

Others with a differing view however argue that the intent, especially these days, may not completely be to keep others down. It may be that those in educational administration never designed and write school books with the intent to help other races, but their own. With that in mind, others have argued hard and blamed other races across the world, saying that they are responsible for their destinies. In other words no one compels them to read those European designed books.

They could take the same ideas, including the scientific ones that tend to be free of opinion and bias write their own textbooks and teach them in ways that will take into account their individual values, cultures, resources and geographical locations. By doing that they could maximize the usefulness of the knowledge. That will help their students find ways to make such knowledge applicable to their special circumstances.

But the argument of Woodson and others is not saying that you should not learn from someone of a different race and geographical location other than yours. What they are saying is, one should not be confined to just that as his community's curricula. For people in Africa and elsewhere, some useful parts of someone's ideas about what materials, subjects, and methods should be taught, should be abandoned for what works for you as a people, and a nation. And that you should be taught about yourself too, and encouraged to generate your own thoughts.

They argue that you should be put on a track to make your own inventions and unique contributions to your unique generation. Woodson for example detested the general mindset education fetches people, no matter how high their educational level is. With the nature of today's curricula, students graduate with a mindset fully designed towards imitating what others have done in the past. "What they have done could be done by others, they contend; and they are right. They are wrong however in failing to realize that what others have done we may not need to do."

And truly if we are to keep imitating what others have done from generations and centuries past, how fast then can we develop solutions for problems of our own times and set our own pace for the upcoming generation. It is akin to impeding progress. We are all human and fully capable of human progress. Every generation has its own geniuses, if they can be equipped with the best educational tools that stimulate their genius and then encourage them to develop their own thoughts, ideas and inventions. Knowledge should be built upon, not stagnant. And so long as the basis of that knowledge is not rooted in your ways and values, it becomes harder for one to adapt to it, or yet still improve on it.

There are contemporary subjects however that tend to be universal in nature. These subjects are not that affected by contemporary curricula in a way that it may become problematic for people of other races and backgrounds that are not Europeans. They include science, math, and technology. But others such as history, literature, philosophy and other art subjects responsible for creativity, social order, analysis and the like are all tainted and at odds with true education for the African.

The results of all the problems enumerated above are many, one being that those who did not really learn what could motivate and help them achieve and live up to their God given potential fail to learn how to earn a living. They come out of schools with the wrong ideology on life. Instead of choosing to enhance their ancestor's local professions or yet innovate to enhance other facets that are needed to develop their communities, they go looking for work from someone else who has done exactly that.

The argument of earlier writers advocating for attitude change is that one should weigh the benefits of approaching learning that takes into account one's own environment as opposed to something one only aspires to become one day, or just wishes for in his imagination. The reality is that contemporary education and its tools and books have been designed to serve a particular people's need and way of life. And these same people, history has shown and recorded, have enslaved and oppressed people they have encountered all across the globe. They have bulldozed every other thought, idea, culture and way of life that is different from theirs and implanted theirs in its place. In some places they have actually obliterated mercilessly the people altogether attempting to annihilate them, as the Native American Indian in the United States, the Aborigines of Australia, etc.

Woodson for example writes that he has found throughout the United States and elsewhere that school drop outs from among the African Americans, who have abandoned school after acquiring the fundamentals of education before indoctrination from manipulated educational curricula, i.e. without graduating high school or reaching college, turn out to be more successful in practically shaping their fate and contributing to their society, than the highly educated college graduate of minority race.

In general he says, college graduates do not contribute to the development of their people. For example, he says, economists from among the African Americans who studied it in schools were taught about Wall Street. They could not use that knowledge to run businesses in their neighborhood. However, immigrants came from without the U S system, learned about the African Americans and moved into their neighborhoods to establish stores and exploit what little money they bring back home from their often menial jobs.

How true today, if you apply it to Nigerian situations also. Graduates linger the streets unable to find a job or start any work they could readily do. It has become so persistent for many years, and not much effort is being made in the right direction to correct it. When universal education was introduced, obligating parents to take school age children for formal education, many parents objected. They argued that the children that have so far benefited them and the society were mostly the ones they trained locally and put to work as carpenters, black and goldsmiths, local textile making and dyeing etc than graduates who sit around doing nothing to benefit themselves or their families. They have failed to connect with their society's demands. Sometimes actually they become a liability, where they end up as drug abusers etc. Those with higher graduate degrees like doctors of Philosophy do not escape either. They become entrapped to few work alternatives and end up cut off from the mainstream of the society, ending up commonly as lecturers.

Without mass campaign that eventually convinces a people that they have to abandon a path they have treaded for years, there is little hope for that change even when Africans themselves take over issues of educational policy and curriculum design. So long as they have been educated within the same foreign institutions abroad, or else foreign influenced institutions within their own countries, there will be no change. This does not negate the fact however, that these people do have the desire to make their communities better, but they are not equipped to "think out of the box." They cannot justify for themselves why they should look for "backwards ideas" as against "modern ones" that defines the idea of progress, affluence and prosperity in the Western sense.

One other area people need to observe in order to protect themselves from predatory education is when a group of people with no interest in their fate or that of their children sit and design their books and curriculum in secret. Then they get some people from among the native population to sit on the board that approves programs to rubber stamp the program in order to give it an apparent legitimacy; i.e. make people think that the people of their race who may have the paper qualification to serve are looking out for their interests. This is one of the most common back door tricks used in many more facets than education alone. So watch out carefully for the kind of people who sits on your educational policy and curriculum departments, to make sure they are truly concerned and will shun temptations to misdirect the education of your children.

Somewhere also, people have to find ways to break the circle of propaganda that has strangled the development of people of color among whom are the Africans on the continent and in the diaspora. The mindset from colonialism and slavery that Africans are backward people, unintelligent, corruptible etc, fueled by the excising of African contribution to the world in the field of science, math, social and economic arena has remained unchanged for centuries. It has become so persistent that today not even Africans will invest in other African businesses. No one goes out of his way, to find a trusting individual running a business to work with him to further enlarge the business for the benefit of the community. Actually the general practice, based on such mindset is to fall victim of headlines from corporate run newspapers that will refuse to allow one to think for himself. Thus he will always endorse those negative headlines with a nod of the head.

Meanwhile the mis-educated person is also a victim of the system and the propaganda it maintains. Unable to fit into a mindset he has adopted, because the door has been shut in his face, and unable to fit into his native community's lifestyle he has been condition to despise, he feels trapped and frustrated. Soon after so much rejection from potential employers, he begins to think himself inadequate. The society he identifies with continues to remind him that he is indeed inadequate. The native community thinks he is either arrogant or incapable of finding a job for himself. Because his formal education did not condition him to think out a strategy, even if it mean he undergoes a intensive program of reversing his thought process, and accepting his former community and its values as worthy, he does not engage in such reversal activities.

In African American communities of the United States today in the 21st century, the neighborhood convenience stores, where you buy basic everyday needs across the street, are owned and operated by foreign immigrants. Other American races feel either that they have better things to do with their lives, or else harbor fear of violence that has become a stereotypical identification of black neighborhoods on media screens, newspapers, theaters, television and radio. They therefore steer clear of African American neighborhoods

In Africa and other communities of African racial people it is no better. No matter how much precious resources, land, and human resources a nation has, the failure to develop the society to a standard commiserate with such resources, is glaringly apparent. They go to their formal schools and graduate with no motivation to work towards common geographical and environmental solutions to their particular problems. Their education was not designed with practical and applicable solutions to those common issues in mind. In commerce for example, they learn about investments and returns on investments on stocks and the like. Their governments, made up of people from the same background are not enthusiastic about serious quests into finding workable alternatives either. So they do not put in place policies that help their local professional trade thrive. Government policies kill their efforts because they are not designed with such common people and their trade in mind, but by textbook theories of what they hope to be.

Also noticed is the need to move away from leadership seeking psyche to service seeking psyche, especially when talking about working within one's native community after acquiring formal education. Acquiring formal education and a degree does not mean you arrogate to yourself the right to only serve in leadership and prominent positions. Whatever entry position you find after graduating, if it would be of service to the people and make things better for your family and community; you have to make a decision to join it without hesitation. It makes your life constructive. It may consequently open the door to gainful employment for you, when you meet the right person while serving, if you are sincere. Many people having returned home from school, become hindrances causing scuffles in neighborhood meetings of organized groups such as the ones set up for local schools and religious institutions. They cause furor over who was elected and who serves as chair, religious leader etc, rather than what is actually being done and how they can contribute to it. Such attitudes scuttle true development. It sometimes pitches one leader against another; or one group against another causing disagreements and crisis, instead of facilitating development.

Feeling inferior with a lower self worth, a consequence of many years of educational race bashing and psychological manipulations that their ancestors have contributed nothing, the educated people of African race feel too ashamed to go back to the farm with new ideas and work their ways to riches. The son of the blacksmith fails to innovate new farm implements, professional, and home tools. He clings to imitation of those that he was taught as being great. Since the great times of African contribution to the world many centuries ago, for example, Africans have gone to school like anyone else, came out with the degrees, but fail to help themselves or their communities.

Because of the failure of our educational systems continent wise, and the failure to genuinely nail or nip such mis-educational problems that still plague our communities, Africans "transfer" technology (from others), not invent any. Though they have resources for all such gadgets like iron and steel, the energy to mould it, the intelligence and various Doctors of Philosophy to research and invent, and the human resources to manufacture. The identified problem of imitation therefore still exists, eighty years after the opinion was first tabled and extensively discussed.

African intellectuals do not study local resources; materials etc and see how they could cheaply provide the same service if not better than those presently adopted for years from Europe as acceptable non changeable culture. For example, as important to every family as housing is, who says we have to build houses out of cement. Even those who taught us that have moved on to other materials that are simple and more economical, and they continue to enhance it every single year. If we had adopted and continue to modify and enhance our local resources that we have in abundance, as used by our ancestors for centuries to build cooler houses in hot climatic areas, and warmer in colder areas, we may have built cheaper more efficient houses. Those houses could cut down on the immense use of electricity for example to cool down houses with corrugated iron roofs that we inherited from colonial days and still use.

All the above are consequences of mis-education, and there are yet still others.

Solutions

From the above, the reader must have figured out that we have to start writing our own textbooks for school use, and be sincere in choosing the right curricula. To date most schools use books that were written with the mindset to teach others that have different values, and therefore are shooting for different stars, lifestyles, and goals. Most of the time, you have a battle on different levels, first with yourself, then your conscience, then your culture, your elders and your people in general in order to even imitate. It becomes a gradual process as more avenues and inventions come before they are incorporated in your own lifestyles. To date for example, desktop computers have not caught on even in richer countries of Africa, decades after its introduction and adoption as a household item in Europe.

Most nations are aware of the problem at some level, but those in leadership fail to work diligently in putting together appropriate textbooks. Such books should choose what part of each subject as being taught today, is of particular importance and relevance to our specific situation, and sift out ones that are not. Then they need to tailor the information and teaching method with specific examples from local events, history, and experience. Other gaps from sifted out sections should be filled with relevant and practical local event that allows for them to know who they are, what their people have done in the past. That will help them build on that foundation with full motivation.

Colleges have to be encouraged to conduct local useful researches looking for information no matter how hard it is to find and record them. They need to concentrate on local issues, local resources and local text and data bases. They have to also knit together such part of historical data, history and literature that have been neglected, lost and disorganized, in order to rewrite from their own perspectives.

And though not excusing local governmental failures, sometimes foreign nations with vested interests in making the world population slaves to their own tastes and ways, for economic and commercial expediency (so they could export to them), send in free donated books convincing them that they do not have to write their own. Nations should resist such temptations. They have to write textbooks at least for the children. Today they are busy filling kids' heads with what hardly helps them. They have to realize the gravity of what they are subjecting their people and the generations to come, slaving for foreign tastes and detesting their own home made goods and tastes. They are mortgaging their lives and the lives of their people, including their children yet unborn.

Country Specific Solutions

Community Participation in Education: Challenges and Prospects in Nigeria.

Dr. I.M. Abbass

Department of Political Science,

Ahmadu Bello University, Zaria.

The current deplorable state of education in Nigeria must be addressed by the whole community, and must not be left to the government alone. The multi dimensional crises in Nigerian educational sector betray very serious failures of government to the community in all ramifications. The crises emerged not due to lack of material and human resources, but primarily on how these resources have been managed or mismanaged to the detriment of the larger members of the community. Hence, serious abuses in the educational sector by government bureaucrats and politicians have assumed one of the greatest crimes committed to humanity. Since the nature and dimension of the educational crises in Nigeria are deeply rooted and cannot be immediately quantifiable, the issue leaves one to conclude with aphorism that 'the more you see, the less you understand' on why the situation defies all solutions or strategies adopted.

Public schools in Nigeria have degenerated beyond limits in terms of physical structures, infrastructure, and the commitment or quality of teachers as well as the concern of authorities in ensuring acceptable standards and the achievement of objectives. Thus, conditions for teaching and learning in public schools have completely deteriorated or even collapsed beyond redemption. Public schools have turned out to be a big liability to the Nigeria educational system but at the same time it has been transformed to conduits through which bureaucrats and politicians have systematically used to siphon funds. While educational standards continue to fall, the schools themselves have been turned into gold mines for politicians.

The greatest tragedy is that government efforts in education are not enough in meeting the needs and aspirations of Nigerians. All these have invariably resulted in the quantitative and qualitative collapse of productive educational pursuits and achievements. Hence, the number of pupils and students turned out yearly are ill prepared for higher education or productive challenges right from the primary to university levels. In other words, performance indicators at all levels of Nigerian educational system have dwindled.

When the Universal Primary Education (UPE) was launched in 1976, for example, there was no adequate plan to achieve the enshrined objectives in all respects and at all levels. These include the projected number of pupils/students, number of schools/classrooms needed, the number and quality of teachers required and other infrastructures and instructional materials. While the UPE was meant to be universal, free and compulsory, it practically did not become free, universal or compulsory, notwithstanding the government public pronouncement and enormous expenditure appropriated. Not all these brought about positive results to the greater community members.

Government's insensitivity to education is largely responsible for the crises. The challenge therefore is that there is a need to have a fundamental reform or shift in the bureaucratic and political behavior in order to have focused, sincere and committed governance with a view to solving such educational crises. In the absence of such deep fundamental reform, the alternative is the evolution of determined community efforts designed to ameliorate the situation. Hence, spirited communities, within the confines of their constituencies should be inspired to address the foreseeable dangers in the interest of the community and to safeguard the qualitative education of their children.

Community Participation: Forms and Dimensions

Participation in general comes in many forms and dimensions, and its nature is that it could manifest in any field of human endeavor like education. Participation could be transitive, moral, free and spontaneous, or otherwise as the case may be. The transitive forms of participation are oriented and designed towards achieving specific objectives. They remain in place and are modifiable, until they achieve those specific goals. However, the type of participation requires an objective application of preventive or healing remedies and must acquire a moral form or desirable perspective without any evil or malicious ends.

Free participation by the affected community of parents, elders, foundations etc, as opposed to forced participation ensures willingness in partaking of operations that are of paramount interest to the community, rather than being forcefully dragged. Tele-guided or manipulated forms of participation, as opposed to spontaneous participation, make the participating community unmotivated.

During the late 1950s, the concept of 'participation' in governance or with other organs/institutions featured prominently in all development programs including education. Thus, the failures of the government programs were attributed to the fact that communities were excluded from the designs, formulations and implementations processes. In order to achieve the desired objectives, there should be a bottom-up and not top-down approach. One has to incorporate the community and their efforts as well as thoughts and ideas in participatory programs.

Lack of community participation has led to project failures in the past and inability to achieve the desired results. Furthermore, new and increasing problems were added without the old ones being solved. The system floundered because communities were not involved in the forms and dimensions of participatory education. Had the community been involved and actively participated in projects, much would have been achieved with much less. Therefore, non-governmental organizations (NGOs) and other spirited groups can bring about fundamental changes in the relationship between government and other stakeholders in the educational and other developmental pursuits.

Hence, in order to achieve more with less, government must adopt participation and participatory methods in governance as a basic policy direction in order to have focus, purpose and relevance. The community likewise must form non-governmental interest groups to stir the government into action, so their loved ones access good quality education. Excessive dependence, centralization and concentration of policy or authority bring about non-participatory planning. It should be noted that social conditions for community participation must always ensure the beneficiary's participation in a number of ways.

In the first place, it must be conceived that people or members of the community are not 'the problem' and bureaucrats/politicians are not 'the solutions'. More often than not, bureaucrats/politicians are the problems, while the people are the solutions. Secondly, the nature and extent of the desired community participation must be unambiguous and acceptable to all stakeholders, right from its initial commencement with clear-cut and achievable objectives. Furthermore, there must be clear and acceptable road map with designs or plans for shared responsibilities at all stages of implementation. Finally, adequate financial commitment and disbursement enshrined with explicit checks and balances must be provided to ensure popular community participation. Furthermore a mechanism for confirming allocation of resources, tracking its use and auditing it, must be open to the public.

Merits of Community Participation in Democracy

Since democracy is the government of the people by the people and for the people, the concept of community participation has, over time, been adopted as a strategic policy by progressive and democratic governments. In the first place, community participation has been transformed as a political slogan. As an attractive political option, government must appreciate the value of participation and how to politically make use of it in the best interest of governance and in league with the community. Participatory devices by government are likely to create feelings of acceptance between government and the community. Therefore, politicians should exploit these situations in order to give their constituencies a sigh of relief and the impression that they are sensitive to people's plights. This is possible and realistic because 'peacefully negotiated forms of participations can take the heat out of many situations where developmental policies create tension and resistance on the part of their victims" (Sachs, 1997:118).

As an instrument of great inspiration to the community and political effectiveness, community participation provides insight knowledge into local activity and reality, which bureaucrats and politicians do not possess. This is because community participation enables the establishment of a network of great and variable ideas and relationships for the government and the community to coexist as well as to make sustained policies succeed satisfactorily.

Not only has participation become a politically designed approach but at the same time an economically attractive proposition. For example, funding and benchmarking must be designed to bring into focus the popular participation of the community in education through investment in the provision of infrastructure, during either economic recession or buoyancy. Government may for example, transfer certain costs in education funding to the community if only there is trust, understanding and harmony between them. Therefore, the community closely links the long-term sustainability of education projects to the active and informed participation it partakes with the government.

The collapse of the UPE in Nigeria could be attributed to the fact that there was no community participation in the program. The Universal Basic Education (UBE) program is equally heading for collapse because of these non-participatory approaches with the community it is supposed to serve. Community participation is no doubt an extraordinarily powerful political and economic policy based tool that has come of age but not effectively utilized to move education out of its present quagmire.

Community participation is no longer a threat to politicians and bureaucrats, provided it is transitive, institutionalized, orderly, morally and freely organized. Therefore, sincere, open and democratic governments, interested in effective community progress, with a desire to achieve more with less, adopt the participatory approach to accomplish the purpose of government. This is in consonance with the desire to strengthen the local communities and modernize national aspirations and needs.

All participatory approaches and strategies are therefore designed to, among others; provide basic infrastructure requirements of education as well as the social and cultural needs of the communities who willingly partake/participate in such designed activities. These empower the communities and make governments legitimately relevant and purposeful everywhere, especially in Nigeria's desperate quest to bring about orderly and democratic participation.

Again, sound and people-oriented educational policies tend to create popular and spontaneous support with induced and addictive need to have a strong public or community participation right from policy-making and implementation as well as how decisions are reached to secure mass community support for government and its programs. Clever governments therefore use communities in a very sophisticated fashion in order to establish control and loyalty over the people. This can only be achieved when governments are not afraid or scared by the outcomes of people's participation in their programs.

As community participation keeps the economy alive and the polity responsive to the community, it should be emphasized that the government's collaborative efforts with communities or NGOs automatically guarantees that government's good image or reputation because such participatory activities or programs involve less bureaucratized approaches and are usually corruption free. This device will invariably bring about the meeting of the needs of the community with greater efficiency, satisfaction and at less cost.

Thus, governments and NGOs should seek to demonstrate keen ability and trust to work together in a participatory fashion with a view to meeting people's aspirations or needs. Government must therefore tilt or bend towards the participatory winds of progress rather than remain sunk within the quicksand of sinking education services so that the current and continuing apathy and protests by the Nigerian people will reduce or even cease. NGOs involved in educational development like Zaria Education Development Association (ZEDA) have expressed readiness to partner with government at all levels to assist in providing services to the community against the private lobbyists who lure bureaucrats and politicians in wasting taxpayers money on education without dividends.

Education and Democratic Participation

Education is a designed act in the transmission of knowledge, information and understanding. This act in itself makes education a fundamental right to everybody. Therefore, the right to education has provided the individual to be empowered and to control the course of his or her life and be respected with dignity. With education, the individual acquires all other rights because it is considered as a precondition for the exercise of all other human rights. In other words, civil and political rights assume relevance, form and substance only when a person is educated.

Since education enhances social mobility up and down the status ladder, and guarantees freedom of individuals from discrimination based on social status, it equally raises community's sense of reasoning and productiveness. As other social and economic parameters are promoted through education, it shows that an educated community has greater opportunities for its members to secure jobs and fulfill other obligations of life. This therefore enables the community to acquire the right or privilege to adequate standard of living for its members with greater access to skills and knowledge needed to productively participate in community and national development. These, no doubt, contribute in accelerating the unity of purpose, which therefore demand that government must make education productively accessible to all, so that no one is directly or indirectly denied the right to education.

There are many connections between education and democratic participation by community members, particularly with regard to the expansion of democratic participation on the one hand and expansion of education on the other (MacEwan, 1999:186). For education to have value or relevance and serve the objectives of the community, it must be organized so that it generates widespread participation amongst its stakeholders. Since education is a primary prerequisite for democratic processes and movements, its relevance is therefore based on the degree of the expansion of democratic participation, which favors the expansion of education.

In other words, education offers and expands an essential entry point as well as a route to the sharing of political power. This means that greater equality in education offers a solid base for democratic power through popular community participation, which also enables the expansion of education and its prevalence within the community. Hence, the ability of the community to effectively participate in democratic process is dependent upon the knowledge, information and understanding its members possess, which is equally dependent on the degree of equality in income distribution in the society as well as the degree of equality in the distribution of education in the community.

Community participation in education, particularly in a democratic system, is very important for the polity as well as for the economy. Since education enhances economic growth, and therefore plays a crucial role in economic strategy, it buttresses that monopoly of education brings about monopoly of power in all its manifestations. The official and predominant structure of Nigerian education system breeds certain implications for the strengthening of the community. Public schools, within the Nigerian educational system, provide avenues through which socialization processes take place, particularly in the development of patriotic citizenry as well as inculcating the right values essential for social cohesion and unity amongst various communities.

Schools therefore form the core contents of the socialization process and thus constitute significant elements in defining the community. Hence, because schools create bonds or connections amongst people through common and shared values, they nonetheless establish links through the set of knowledge imparted and other forms of social practices put in place. Another vital form of the school-community relations is the extent to which community members are directly involved in the governance of the schools. Thus, when students' parents and other members of the community take active roles in the various aspects of the school's operations, the standard and quality of education is likely to significantly improve. These roles may include everything from curriculum planning to hiring and firing of teachers, to fund-raising and planning of the schools social activities.

One of the most fundamental issues bordering on participation is the nature, form and substance of integration approaches or devices the schools adopt with the community. For example, are the schools drawing their students and strength from the immediate geographical surroundings or from a larger area? Whatever the case may be, the schools are expected to be integrated with the community on either platform. In essence, the impact of schools on the community will largely depend on the strengthening of the community based on the established bonds, as well as on how the schools system are organized and the degree to which they are organically integrated with the community needs and aspirations.

Such integrations will also improve the standard, quality and image of the school partly because the parents and other members of the community have in-depth knowledge and understanding of the problems and needs of the schools as well as the ability of the students, which they all collectively and willingly bring into the schools as additional values. All these, no doubt, facilitate the work of the teachers and administrators in significant ways. Such integrations and connections between the school and the community create an emotional bond and involuntary reflexes amongst students who feel involved about the school as theirs and to protect the institution as their own. This sense of 'ownership' provides the motivating factor for scholarship and competitions amongst students, which invariably enhances education and promotes the community.

School-community connections must be vigorously pursued and developed in order to significantly improve the schools as well as strengthen the community. Such connection also ensures that other elements in the participatory approaches and democratic development strategy are all combined together for the enhancement of education through community participation. Since direct community participation in education builds integral and sustainable linkages, which at the same time strengthens democratic practices, the community invariably exercises power through participation, which leads to easy accessibility to education, economic growth and popular support for the government.

Conclusion

Community initiative along with government sensitivity and responsibility to education are vital to community participation in education. The continued marginalization of the community by government, through bureaucrats and politicians, by the gimmick promises to provide education should motivate the community to press or agitate for a policy shift. Government should therefore adopt participatory alliances, as an institutionalized policy, in league with community development associations in order to save education from further crises and decay. Hence, the type of interactions that should ensure community-government league in education are designed to prevent further deterioration in the provision of education with a view to giving new scenarios for enhanced grassroots participation so as to generate people's satisfaction in all spheres of human endeavors. In essence, community participation in education must remove all obstacles that hinder access to education by giving the community unlimited opportunity and indeed the right to activity and directly participate in all facets of educational activities. This reflects the fact that expanded education brings greater democratic power to the community, which equally generates equality and in turn provides a foundation for justice, equity and fairness amongst all spectrum of humanity.

Chapter Nine

Revisiting the Status of Women

Introduction

It is with great humility, and not malice that I set out to write about what has turned out to be a great part of my contribution to my community as a broadcast journalist. As a young Muslim woman who started an International broadcasting career at the age of 26, I chose to produce a weekly feature titled "Family," to enable me work on dealing with some of the struggles in the life of multitudes of women trying hard to contribute within their families and communities. I have come to understand after almost twenty years producing that weekly feature for international broadcast to West Africa from the United States that most issues that negatively impact on our families in general relate to the unjust position and limitations ascribed to the womenfolk within the relationship. These are some of the issues that I would like to share with the public, especially Muslims, whom it affects primarily.

From the onset, I would like my readers to understand that this is not a fight, vendetta, or fault finding work just for the sake of it; far from that. I just realized that to ignore some wrongs one sees everyday just because one may be assigned one label or another for speaking out against it, is not a viable option for me. And as a wife and mother, to fight men is to fight the people I love, my father, brothers, husband and male children. So this is in good faith to allow us look at ourselves with an objective mind in order to find solutions, where needed, to right some of the wrongs. Today I am concentrating on the treatment of women among Islamic communities across the world.

Premise

To discuss how Islam as a religion views women in general, and to do that effectively, one has to confine his search to the text of the Quran as the leading source and guide for all Muslims. Where one does not have an explicit verdict from the text of the Quran itself, then one goes to the second source of guidance to all Muslims, the Hadith (compiled works) (of) Sunnah (way of life and practice) of our teacher the prophet. Ahadith (plural) have been accepted as important second source of guidance because the Prophet of Islam was not only sent with a message from God, but has been charged to guide and set example for his followers. "In him you have a prefect example" says the Holy Quran.

So Prophet Muhammad's (pbuh) sayings, actions and verdicts in life have been followed carefully and documented for additional guidance to the Muslim. And of course his verdicts do not contradict, but further explains and puts into practice the words, rules and laws of God documented in the Quran. Apart from these two sources however, Muslims as a group have been influenced by as much practices that relates to women as there are cultural differences between the many countries of the world where the Islamic population of one thousand five hundred million (1.5 billion) reside.

The Persistence of Arab cultural relegation of Women

Early Islamic teachings in Arabia brought revolutionary changes to the life and culture of its immediate adherents, the Arabs. Some of the most remarkable changes affect the question of justice and equality among the diverse community of Muslims. After just a few decades of Islamic propagation, the warring Arabs were peaceful and compassionate to each other. The two main groups from the status quo that were affected by that change were women and slaves.

Though there still exists gender difficulties and problems that need addressing to bring the community of Muslims to the level propagated by the Prophet of Islam and its Holy Book, some Muslim countries are more adoptive of the teachings and quite ahead than others, again mainly based on different cultural backgrounds. Before Islam, it was not only slaves who were viewed by the inhabitants of Arabia as property; women were also viewed the same way. And the main reason behind that was not just that Arabs were inherently barbaric, they were engaged in excessive clan loyalty coupled with commerce with passion, something akin to capitalism of today where in its excessive grip sometimes humane policies of caring for the weak is trampled upon.

What made the Arabian situation worse however was that they were engaged in family and clan feud that usually lasted for generations. Blood letting based on familial enmity were very common. As such wars were fought almost all the time. War became so excessive that the

Arabs by themselves decided to enter into truce for at least some months of the year. That allowed them some time to plan activities that were important and also those that ensured their progress. It also ensured safe passage to commercial caravans, as well as visitors to the Holy Kaaba (then in the custody of pagans). It was through such wars that captives from the enemy or opposing clans were taken and kept in bondage at homes and businesses to engage in services of various kinds based on the gender of the captives. Since these captives were naturally long time enemies to the captors, sometimes handed over to expiate the murder of a relative they have committed, they were not generally treated well.

Women were not treated well either. They were not viewed with value and dignity, so much so that at about the time Islam began to be preached, men were burying their infant girls alive, viewing the birth of a female child as something to be embarrassed about, or worse still, a curse. Women entertained men in all capacities at brothels, including dancing almost naked at drinking and gambling pubs, just like what you may have watched in Western movies depicting the Wild West of the United States, in the early years of immigration of Europeans to the American continent.

The Effect of Islam in Arabia

Islam did a remarkable job in weeding out immoral and unethical behaviors, and achieving some uniformity and bonding based on faith principally. Islam permeated other sectors of life as well such as doing away to a great extent with blood feuds between clans. The easing of blood feuds gradually eased captives taking and consequently slavery began to wane. Islam also began to resolve many judicial cases by the act of freeing slaves still in bondage. Such edicts concerned cases of murder, breaking an oath that one has committed to; and some other situations. Soon the slaves already taken were being freed. Finally Islam enjoined principles of treating ones slaves. For example, one has to dress a slave with the same quality material used within the family he serves. Likewise, one was not supposed to ask a man in bondage to cook high class food for the master and people of the household, while the cook eat some low class food. The food the family ate should also be what people under bondage eat.

Writing about women in his book on the four Imams that were responsible for the four schools of thoughts in Islam, Aftab Shahryar states:

> *"The men were prepared to accept Islam as a revolution in relations in public life, an overturning of political and economic policies....but they did not want Islam to change anything concerning relations between the sexes."*
> *"While slavery affected only the wealthy, the change in the status of women, (their right to inherit for instance) affected all."*[8]

So though there were remarkable changes to the way of life of the average Arab in Mecca, Medina and cities between the two, with the advent and early growth of Islam, some changes were harder to swallow. I will discuss two.

The most important of these Islamic reforms that became difficult to adopt in my opinion was the outright denial of community leadership based on knowledge and piety as taught by Islam, leaning instead towards lineage and inheritance. Soon after the passing of the Holy Prophet, the culture of clan loyalty soon overshadowed and overturned knowledge and piety as a criteria. The study of Islam however, and the example set by the Prophet himself will clearly show that leadership in Islamic community should be based on knowledge and piety. The Quran makes it clear time and time again; that Allah does not take into account the wealth, position, possession, gender, ethnicity, race, lineage, language or any other factor to rank people in His acceptance of their level or grade with Him. He clearly states in the Quran that the best of us is one that obeys His laws the most. So in Islam the most knowledgeable and pious should lead, not the son of so and so.

As stated earlier, before Islam, family lineage was a strong custom where the ordinary Arab will easily tell you his lineage by hundreds of years. So soon after the four immediate companions of the Prophet of Islam

---

[8] Shahryar, A (2003) "Legacy of the four Great Imams" New Delhi: Islamic Book Service P.40

held the title of Amirul Mu'minin (Leaders of the faithful), the Arabs went back to the system of leadership through inheritance or lineage. In fact three of the four earlier Caliphs of Islam, his immediate disciples and the closest people who lived with him, met untimely death through assassination. That demonstrates how strongly the feudal customary institutions were and their determination to prevail under any circumstances. The resulting rebellion to piety as the key to leadership resulted in the acceptance of the monarchy we witness today in most Islamic countries.

Women also suffered the same fate. A reversal of their position started no sooner than the passing away of the Messenger of Allah. When the Prophet was living among the Muslim Community, women's image had been raised to a position whereby they were treated with dignity. Women at the time of the Holy Prophet were actively involved in both religious and public work. The wives of the prophet and other socially active women were known to have contributed to humanitarian work on battlefields, nursing the wounded, cooking the food for the forces, and supplying needed amenities.

Women were engaged in commerce, and kept properties and wealth in their own maiden names. In fact the Prophet's first wife Khadija was a wealthy commercially engaged woman. Their life together, while she controls such vast wealth never came between her and the Messenger of Allah. That was how simple and humble the Prophet was. He was neither jealous nor overbearing just because his wife is known to the public to be the wealthy one in their marital home. In fact because of her status, she provided some from of security for him against his enemies within the community. His life with his first wife Khadija was related as the most peaceful and satisfactory to the Prophet, such that he never took a second wife while she was alive, and would probably not have even after her but for the persistence of his companions and relatives who continue to watch him caring for his children alone, and suggested he takes in Saudah, a widow who might help him with raising and caring for the children. At that time he was already about fifty years old.

The Prophet not only taught during his lifetime that it was important to educate the women folk, he explained why. They are the first teachers for the formative years of the children, and naturally more involved in the upbringing of the children within any normal family. He treated his women with care and esteem. For example, though the Prophet himself led a very simple life, his wives Ummahat-al-Mu'minin were in a class of their own. While traveling they were usually mounted on rides enclosed in a mini tent while such camels were usually led by Muslim men on foot. That was why, as related while on one of such travels when Aisha (*Rathiyallahu Anha*) went looking for a jewelry she dropped, the caravan left without her, under the assumption that she was in the enclosure on the mount.

Aftab cites occasions where some of the earliest ahadith on women were misrepresentations, deliberate or otherwise (Allah knows best). One of such hadith reported in Bukhari collections by just one narrator Abu Bakra (Vol. 9 Book 88 number 219) is responsible for most of the position that people take today to suppress women participation in legitimate issues of concern to them, their family, and community in general. Many people including scholars who lean towards Arab cultural prejudices use the Hadith to deny leadership positions to women, though they do know that the credibility of Abu Bakra the narrator has been challenged by *Amirul Mu'minin* Umar Bin Khattab himself. Other negative Ahadith about women were also challenged by others including the Prophet's wife Aisha (Rathiyallahu Anha).

Aftab writes that the Hadith came from an unreliable narrator named Abu Bakra; the same Abu Bakra that was reported to have been flogged by Caliph Umar for false testimony. Abu Bakra was reported to have attributed to the Prophet of Islam (SAW) the following. "Those who entrust their affairs to a woman will never know prosperity." It is today mostly on the basis of that single hadith that women in the Islamic world are denied political participation.

Another incident recounted by Aftab Shahryar demonstrates how even at the time when the Prophet's widow Aisha (RA) was alive, some were transmitting questionable and negative ahadith in relation to women. When told about what Abu Huraira transmitted as having been said by the Prophet of Islam that "the dog, the donkey and a woman interrupt prayer if they pass in front of the believer, interposing themselves between him and the Qibla" she recounted (reported by Ibn Marzaq) "You compare us now to asses and dogs. In the name of God, I have seen the Prophet saying his prayers while I was there, lying on the bed between him and the Qibla. And in order not to disturb him I did not move." Bukhari, the most authentic source of hadith also recorded the same hadith from Aisha with some moderations in his book of prayers. You can find the Hadith including online; they are in Bukhari Book 9, ahadith numbers 493 and 498.

The notion from earlier religions before Islam that a woman is evil who ate the apple, thus labeling the first women Eve is erroneous. Or other sources who say she was the one who tempted Adam have all been thrown out by the Islamic version of the event. In Islam both male and female have a propensity or choice towards good or evil, and that the whole idea of living on earth is to test our resilience in repelling evil and striving towards good. Both sexes are accountable for their actions, both here and the hereafter, with no discrimination.

If we observe the Islamic verses more closely, the Creator of us all did not derogate the woman. In his book (Badawi, 1995) *"Gender and Equality in Islam: Basic Principles"* Jamal Badawi the writer explains that:

> *"the Quran neither blames the woman for the fall of man (human family), nor accepts the argument or belief that she is being punished for her original sin, (eating from the forbidden tree) through menstruation and child birth. On the contrary, in Islam the Mother is revered and given a degree threefold more than the father in status with the children, for her childbearing and care."*

The Quran did not in any of its verses assign blame on Hauwa (Eve) for the fall of the two.

Actually, just for the sake of clarity, according to a verse of the Quran it was Adam that received the whisper of Satan during the tempting incident. Let us be clear here that we are not assigning blame on Adam either, just bringing out the Quranic facts. Allah has the best knowledge as to the details of what happened, and people should be careful about condemning women a half of human creation under false or assumptive notions. The Quran says (Quran 20:120) "But Satan whispered evil to him, he said O Adam shall I lead thee...." The next verse says "With the result that they both ate of the tree." With the same spirit of non-partisanship and justice as it relates to Allah's messages in the Quran, Allah equally rebuked both for having disobeyed His words.

Right next to the incident, as related by Quran in Islam, you will also learn that both were forgiven for the incident. Most verses addressed both. The prayer after realizing what has happened was also reported to be uttered by both (7:23) "They said: "Our Lord we have wronged our own souls, if Thou forgive us not and bestow not upon us Thy mercy, we shall certainly be lost." Addressing humans after that Allah says immediately in relation to the above "O ye son of Adam let not Satan seduce you, in the same manner as he got your parents out of the garden...." Allah could have mentioned just Adam but He made reference to both (parents).

Another pointer is, almost all commandments to a believer in the Holy Quran begin with a common address (Medani Surahs) *Ya aiyuhal lathina amanu* "O you who believe" (regardless of gender) addressing the community of Muslims altogether. Some verses actually take the time to name both and address them equally in relation to what was being said. "Believing men and believing women, men who keep pure and women who keep pure." In Islam both male and female are entitled to equality before the law.

Punishment for breaking the law falls on both genders, so also commandments for righteousness. Examples are the punishment for theft, (Quran 5:38) fornication (Quran 24:2) murder and injury (Quran 5:45). Finally a whole chapter was titled Suratul Nisa the chapter of Women (Chapter Four). In it were specified detailed rights of relationship, marriage and others. Here it does not appear that men were neglected with no chapter of their own because they were less important than women, far from that. It is more reasonable to think it is against the backdrop of the situation within the society regarding the treatment of women that Islam and its book the Holy Quran took the time to relate guidance as it relates to such relationships. *Asbab-al Nuzul* (the reasons for revelations) teaches as part of the science of revelations in Islamic scholarship, that incidents and circumstances prevalent within the society do instigate the revelation of verses.

Further study of the Quranic parables and lessons will also show us the role of women and their virtues. The first woman was created to provide companionship to the first man in the garden. And so also in the grand design of our Creator, in the mysteries of living things on the whole planet, we find animals and plants existing in pairs. Reproduction in the human and animal world goes in pairs. The necessity for one to complement the other is readily apparent in the design of the Creator. That is what we were made for. In order to multiply and be what God wants us to be, both parents need to pitch in. Only then can we fully impart the right lessons and set example for the children thereby ensuring better generations of believers of both sexes.

Arabs through the lessons of Islam for the first time in a long while recognized the dignity of a woman, giving her rights to inheritance. For that reason, especially in Arabia, women began to keep their family name even after marriage in order to continue to hold titles to their property. Islam was very kind to the woman in matters of material possessions. In Islam, a woman is not obligated to spend anything from her personal property on the household within which she is married into, unless she chooses to. Some scholars however stress that in instances where the husband is sick or incapacitated in some way, it is only fair that she steps up to help. This still is at her discretion, as Islam did not obligate her.

Badawi (1995) says "there is no text in the Quran or Sunnah that precludes women from any position of leadership, except in leading prayer."[9] Abdullahi Yusuf Ali too, the most popular translator and commentator (*Mufassir*) of the Quran in modern times, in discussing the question of gender equality, was very clear on the fact that the difference is not significant, and has a reason behind it. In Surah Al-Imran (Quran 3:195), for example, where Allah says "**Never will I suffer to be lost the work of any of you, be he male or female, you are from one**

---

[9] **Badawi, J. (1995) Gender Equality in Islam: Basic Principles Plainfield: American Trust Publications P. 38**

another;" Abdullahi Yusuf Ali in his translation of the Quran (The Meaning of the Quran) commented thus: (commentary number 500 Pg. 180) *"In Islam the equal status of the sexes is not only recognized but insisted on. If sex distinction in nature does not count in spiritual matters, still less of course would count artificial distinctions such as rank, wealth, position, race, color, birth etc."* His interpretation shows clearly that the path to Allah is the same for both the male and the female, in worship or service. And because in spiritual matters which matter the most in the religious domain, Allah has placed responsibilities on both sexes, no one should block women from performing such responsibilities which are actually Allah's commandments. Other scholars also have voiced similar positions. For example, many scholars cite the role of Umm Salamah at a very difficult time for the Muslims during the treaty of Hudaibiyah, when the Prophet of Islam was prevented by the Pagan Meccans from performing Umrah, and many Muslims were agitated.

At Hudaibiyah, Umm Salamah played a critical role to diffuse the tension, a role equivalent today to the Chief advisor of the Head of State. Also during the life of the Prophet of Islam, not only were intelligent women acknowledged by the Prophet, some were by Allah Himself, as in the case of the woman for which a whole chapter of the Quran was named Mujadilah (The woman who disputed). God revealed verses in connection to the woman, with Allah siding with her concern.

Women should not be shunned in economic, political and social processes of their society. It is quite clear that in Islam the only basis of superiority are piety and knowledge. Regardless of whether one is male or female, the leader should be the most pious and knowledgeable, piety being the leading quality (i.e. being more loyal and attuned to Allah's commandments as against one's selfish desires). Such a person is the most befitting of respect and leadership regardless of gender. At these times when the men folk have generally failed their societies and have formed a very counterproductive political culture, it is probably the best time to open the door for capable women.

Conclusion

People should seriously move away from coining lies against the teachings of Allah and His apostle and selling it as part of religion. One has to be very careful today, not to fall victim or be misled by a deeply rooted cultural bias, as against what Allah and the Prophet established. While some people have knowingly use Islam to profess their inner prejudices and cultural norms, some overshadowed by their cultural practices devoid of Islamic guidance blindly and sometimes unconsciously mislead others. We need to be alert and conscious of all interpretations. If in doubt of an issue, ask the person relating it for the source of that law or rule. Cross check it before you engage in it.

It is very important for the growth, strength, and development of Muslim communities that they bring to fold the contribution of women to their family and community. Asian and African Islamic countries appear to be way ahead of Arab countries in women participation in community development and leadership. Some Islamic countries such as Bangladesh and Pakistan have had women Head of States. Iran, and to some extent Kuwait, are way ahead of say Saudi Arabia. A lot more has to be done, and culture versus religion has to be identified as such, and credibly challenged for any meaningful progress to occur.

To neglect half of one's community in matters and issues relating to development is tantamount to a human being who refuses the gift of both hands that Allah provided him, choosing to use just one to accomplish everything, every single day. It means you progress at a very slow pace, literally half the rate at which you should progress. It is all the more important today, though it has always been, that Muslims respect each and every verse of the Quran, including those that may not be comfortable to their way of life and customs. I have heard many dedicated Muslims from both genders give positive lectures about the issue, but it appears the pace at which the community is changing its practices as it relates to women leaves much to be desired. May Allah guide us all and make it easy for us to do His will. (Amen)

Chapter Ten

Revamping Strategies for African Economies

Hadiza Wada, DBA

Dateline: August 7, 2009

The current economic order globally is unsustainable. For continued co-existence, every nation has to be a participant, whether a major producer or a consumer. This demands, at the bare minimum, adequate ability to be either. Though the industrialized nations continue to hold the financial key to the realization of most developmental projects, and also the production of goods, the consuming nations have to be strong enough to continue to afford buying products or services from them.

Everything around us is however failing at a fast rate, be it the physical condition of the earth itself, where we face problems of global warming, ice cap melting at the poles, devastating tsunami not seen in a very long time, and highly devastating hurricanes. Then there is the increasing greed of the industrialized nations which has become so much of a problem even before the current financial market crisis.

The cause for global poverty, disease, and deaths according to various sources, lies with the IMF and World Bank's strangling policies on the one hand, and unfair global trade policies on the other. Both arrangements benefit the industrialized at the expense of the developing nations. Both sides however are now sure that the result of continuing along the same path is suicidal. The approach to what needs to be done is what differentiates the victim of the current order, as against its perpetrators.

G8 Initiates actions in panic

Just before the turn of the century, some common problems reached critical level. The consuming nations have been so much strangled that the industrialized nations began to panic, and there is a reason for that panic. If history is something we can learn from, the panic does not appear to be out of moral sound judgment, but primarily because those burdened nations are crashing under the weight of debt, and may not have a healthy market for buying and consuming their industrialized goods. Many nations at that time, and even now, have been choosing between basic health care and food for their citizens, dying daily from poverty and basic curable diseases. That precipitated a rush for the first time, at a meeting of the G8 in Gleneagles to consider debt relief and write-offs. The ripple effect of such realization and ensuing panic did not stop however, until today even the industrialized nations are beginning to exhibit the same global problems of the developing nations.

Debt relief and write-offs are just a band-aid procedure on a wound that needs proper medication, attention and care to heal. The relief may have also come too late to do much good. Serious transformation is necessary. Many concerned NGOs and movements across the globe have decried the policies and practices that led the world into such dilemma. They advocated a different approach to policies that clearly indicate the way global economic and trade policies are running headlong into a devastating crash to everyone's detriment.

In his book which he dedicated to those committed to creating a stable, sustainable, and peaceful world, John Perkins (2007), who was an official agent of corporations involved in corporate scams, exposed many tactics, usually ruthless, engaged in by multinational corporations, financial institutions and world's powerful governments to create and sustain an imbalanced system of global trade, financing, and ultimately domination of their lives and economy. Perkins believes that effective reform ideas should be generated and discussed, studied, analyzed and implemented directly at corporate level. Also urgently needed are an active population in the United States especially, and other countries across the globe, pushing their governments for trade policy changes, including scrutiny of their tax dollars used in those "multi billion dollar scams." He goes on to say that modern corporations have all the rights of individuals "under current laws of the United States, but none of the responsibilities. In fact, they are licensed to steal."

It is important here to differentiate from the people in the West, ordinary hard working individuals who are the tax payers whose taxes fund governmental programs. These average people sometimes further donate for private charitable works, from their already taxed income. They however are not aware of the counter productive policies and practices that those they entrust with their money at governmental level engage in.

The Crux of the matter

The World Bank and International Monetary Fund, IMF, according to various researches, collaborate with corporations to entrap poor nations endowed with resources the corporations crave, by generating loans they know the poor countries could not keep up with the payment. They then later on accuse those countries of violating the repayment terms, adding penalty after penalty in money terms, further ballooning the debt. It was one of the causes that saw massive demonstrations by activists and NGOs in industrialized countries beginning about a decade ago, including one that forced the closure of World Trade Organization (WTO) meeting in Seattle in December of 1999. Since 1999 to date, demonstrators from different countries continue to disrupt WTO meetings wherever they are held, decrying among other things the policies of the IMF, World Bank, international trade and industrialized nations.

But, how bad are those "scams" that Perkins is talking about:

> *"We channeled funds from the bank and its sister organizations into schemes that appeared to serve the poor, while primarily benefiting a few wealthy people. Under the most common of these, we would identify a developing country that possessed resources our corporations coveted (such as oil), arrange a huge loan for that country, and then direct most of the money to our own engineering and construction companies – and a few collaborators in the developing country."*

Giles Bolton (2008), a foreign aid agent, however initiated his position by describing the failures in three areas of African development that he would rather hold Africa or its governments responsible. They are corruption, conflict, and lack of democracy. All three, he says, are primarily internal problems. He only holds foreign governments and corporations as accomplices. That statement however is arguable to many who know better. But Bolton does agree however, with Perkins's position that the donors and aid packaging experts generally spend money on badly conceived and targeted projects, with no real impact on the receiving nations' population. Areas he stressed are low interest loans and grants (aid) where he enumerated some of the problems as; having little or no honest public debate about the quality of aid, thereby keeping foreign public in the dark about persistent bad aid. The result is more money spent badly.

However, as commonly misunderstood by most people around the globe about the use of aid funds in African countries, Bolton says corruption or misappropriation of foreign aid from tax payers is an insignificant percentage, if at all. Why? Aid is carefully planned and targeted to specific programs. The money released is tied to continuous monitoring of the funds, and regular audits are conducted thereafter. If doubts exist, aid is interrupted at will by donor.

Bolton also supports Perkins premise that one of the most devastating policies and practices that resulted in the current African economic crisis was created and nourished by the World Bank and IMF. Skyrocketing interest rates and bad economic policies, loans with little regard for ability to pay back etc consequently led to defaulting in repayment. He goes on to give a vivid description of the exploitation that resulted from it:

> *"Many African countries continued to default, and saw their debt rise and rise. Nigeria, for example, originally borrowed $5 billion from foreign governments and institutions; although it had since paid back $16 billion, in early 2006 it still owed $32 billion more."*

Then there is the question of the structures through which global trade occurs, whether they give an equal (or fair) chance to the world's poor countries. Apart from subsidies to local farmers in the US and those to cattle farmers in the EU, which continues to devastate African farmers, there is another enduring problem. A carefully crafted game of defrauding the producers at developing countries was an ancient art that others find acceptable to follow.

Bolton explains that an unfair and morally unjust practice which began long ago during colonial times, for example, saw Britain banning cotton processing in India, a century old practice by Indians. The same cotton from India was then exported cheaply to Industries built in England to receive, process the cotton, weave them into clothes, and then sell them internally within Britain and abroad to other countries including India.

Solutions to the problems

Perkins sees no option but to transform all these problem areas, using genuine policies and practices. That will ensure an enduring relationship as common citizens of a single planet. Globalization has presently led to constant around the clock mass movement of people, goods, ideas etc across nations. Long gone are the days of policies of greed and selfishness in such matters; choosing to protect only one's people, their health and ideas to the detriment of, or at the expense of others on the same planet. This has been amply demonstrated today by issues such as the pattern of the spread of Swine Flu, proliferation of the use of world-wide-web to retrieve information on almost anything, and corporate outsourcing of manufacturing and services globally, etc. It has also been demonstrated economically and financially by the global effect of the recent Wall Street (market) crisis from the late 2009 in the United States.

How does one confront the problems, and where will one start to implement solutions? Perkins advocated transforming the trend and creating a world the upcoming generation will be proud to inherit. This we do through "transformation of the power-base of the corporatocracy, the corporations – the way they define themselves, set their goals, develop methods for governance, and establish criteria for selecting their top executives." Possible? Yes, he says. He goes on to provide examples of times when people rose to change past practices and succeeded in making changes to corporate practices through compelling campaigns and actions, e.g. movement against environmental pollution, ozone layer depletion etc.

The power base for forcing those changes lies with the people. The fact that the people in general make and bring down governments through the ballot, provide the manpower into manufacturing, and also are the consumers of corporate products, is the key to success. It essentially means people are the power behind corporate endeavors. The general population therefore holds the critical tools for corporate survival, and can use it with enough campaign and awareness to enforce changes.

References by Chapters

Chapter One

1. Carew, J. (1988) African Presence in the Americas: Fulcrum of Change. New Jersey: African World Press, Inc.

2. Diop, C. A. (1991) Civilization or Barbarism: An Authentic Anthropology. Brooklyn: Lawrence Hill Books.

3. Norton, P. B. & Esposito, J. J. (1994) Egypt. Chicago: Encyclopaedia Britannica, Inc. Vol. 18, P 91-154

4. Sertima, I. V. (1976) They Came Before Columbus: The African Presence in Ancient America. New York: Random House.

Chapter Two

5. Murray, S. (2007, July 2) *The dying factories of Kano* BBC News, Africa. http://news.bbc.co.uk/2/hi/africa/6245448.stm

6. Ogunbayo, M. (2009, September 27) *The Fall of the Giant* Newswatch Magazine.

7. Sani, B. M. & Sulaiman, S. *The Structure of Kano Economy* Kano: Kano forum www.kanoonline.com

8. Yusuf, B. (2008, May 8) Nigeria: "Essay" on reviving the textile http://www.agoa.info/?view=.&story=news&subtext=919

9. Nigeria Loses industries to Ghana, *People's Mandate* Monthly.

Chapter Three

10. Denja, Y. (January 11, 1999) *Environmental Rights Action: Oil Watch Africa.*

Chapter Nine

30. Badawi, J. (1995) Gender Equality in Islam: Basic Principles Plainfield: American Trust Publications, P. 38.

31. Shahryar, A (2003) Legacy of the four Great Imams. New Delhi: Islamic Book Service, P.40.

Chapter Ten

32. Giles Bolton (2008) Africa Doesn't Matter: How the West Has Failed the Poorest Continent and What We Can Do About It. New York: Arcade Publishing.

33. John Perkins (2007) The Secret History of the American Empire: Economic Hit Men, Jackals, and the Truth about Global Corruption. New York: Penguin Group.

leaders <u>1998 Yearbook of theNational Council of Professors of School Administration</u> Economics Press

21. Hughes, R., Ginnett, R., & Curphy, G. (2002). Leadership: Enhancing the Lessons of Experience. New York: McGraw-Hill/Irwin

22. French, J. R. P., Raven, B. The bases of social power. In D. Cartwright and A. Zander (Eds.) (1959) Group dynamics. New York: Harper & Row.

23. Roach, C. F, & Behling, O. (1984). Leaders and managers: International perspectives on managerial behavior and leadership. In J. G. Hunt et al (Eds.). New York: Pergamon.

Chapter Eight

24. Abbass, I.M and Babajo, A.K. (Eds.) (2003) The Challenge of Community Participation in Education. PTI Press Effurun.

25. Erazo, X; Kirkwood, M; Vlaming, F (Eds.) (1996) Academic Freedom 4: Education and Human Rights. Zed Books, London.

26. Cernea, M. M. (Ed.) (1985) Putting People First: Sociological Variables in Rural Development. Oxford University Press, New York.

27. MacEwan, A. (1999) New Liberalism or Democracy? Economic Strategy, Markets and Alternatives for the 21st Century. Zed Books, London.

28. Sachs, W. (Ed.) (1997) The Development Dictionary, A Guide to knowledge as Power. Zed Books, London.

29. Woodson, C. G. (1990) The Mis-Education of the Negro. Washington D.C.: The Associated Publishers, Inc.

11. Hassan, M. K. (October, 2009) *Energy Crisis and Solutions*: A paper. presented at the Optimist Conference.

12. International Energy Agency, Retrieved (December, 2009) from `http://www.iea.org`

13. Mbendi Information Services, Retrieved (December, 2009) from `http://www.mbendi.com/indy/oilg/ogrf/f/p0005.htm`

14. UNIDO: Regional Center for Small HydroPower, Abuja: Retrieved (December, 2009) from `http://unidorc.org/nigeria/default.htm`

15. Wikipedia: Hydro Power. Retrieved (December, 2009) from `http://www.green-trust.org/hydro.htm`

Chapter Six

16. Hills, A. *Police commissioners, presidents and the governance of Security* (September, 2007) *The Journal of Modern African Studies*, Vol. 45, no. 3 (Pgs 403 – 423)

17. Ibrahim, J., (2003) *Democratic Transition in Anglophone West Africa* Dakar, Senegal: Council for the development of Social Sciences. www.codesria.org.

18. Klantschnig, G. *The politics of law enforcement in Nigeria* (December 2009) *The Journal of Modern African Studies* Vol. 47, no. 4 (Pg. 524 – 549)

Chapter Seven

19. Bass, R. (1984) The Bass Handbook of Leadership: Theory, Research, and Managerial Applications. New York: Simon and Schuster

20. Danzig, A., & Porter, C. (1998) Can leadership be taught? What is learned from writing and analyzing the stories of education

www.ingramcontent.com/pod-product-compliance
Lightning Source LLC
Chambersburg PA
CBHW032251150426
43195CB00008BA/406